'The ultimate guide to a better you. A fascinating and inspiring read.'
Mo Gawdat

'Packed with lived experiences and intuitive ideas. A very entertaining read that had me chuckling away many times! I highly recommend it.'
Stuart White, CEO, HSBC Global Asset Management

'Ryan Hopkins combines his trademark sense of humour with a pragmatic view of wellbeing, making this an engaging and informative read.'
Clare Fernandes, Chief Medical Officer, BBC

'This is a book we all need, with facts conveyed through the prism of someone who has lived life hard, fully, and come through with all the love in the world.'
Carmel McConnell MBE, tech entrepreneur and author

'A book of bite-sized bits of brilliance. Dip in or read it all at once – the choice is yours. Ryan Hopkins has set out the micro-interventions and habit changes that will improve your working life.'
Isabel Berwick, *Financial Times*

T0025794

52 WEEKS OF WELLBEING

A no-nonsense guide
to a fulfilling work life

Ryan Hopkins

KoganPage

First published in Great Britain and the United States in 2024 by Kogan Page Limited

2nd Floor, 45 Gee Street	8 W 38th Street, Suite 902	4737/23 Ansari Road
London	New York, NY 10018	Daryaganj
EC1V 3RS	USA	New Delhi 110002
United Kingdom		India
www.koganpage.com		

Kogan Page books are printed on paper from sustainable forests.

© Ryan Hopkins, 2024

ISBNs
Hardback	978 1 3986 1393 5
Paperback	978 1 3986 1391 1
Ebook	978 1 3986 1392 8

British Library Cataloguing-in-Publication Data
A CIP record for this book is available from the British Library.

Library of Congress Cataloging-in-Publication Data
Names: Hopkins, Ryan, author.
Title: 52 weeks of wellbeing : a no-nonsense guide to a fulfilling work life / Ryan Hopkins.
Description: London ; New York, NY : Kogan Page Inc, 2024. | Includes bibliographical references.
Identifiers: LCCN 2023043833 (print) | LCCN 2023043834 (ebook) | ISBN 9781398613911 (paperback) | ISBN 9781398613935 (hardback) | ISBN 9781398613928 (ebook)
Subjects: LCSH: Quality of work life. | Work–Psychological aspects. | Well-being.
Classification: LCC HD6955 .H637 2024 (print) | LCC HD6955 (ebook) | DDC 650.1–dc23/eng/20231101
LC record available at https://lccn.loc.gov/2023043833
LC ebook record available at https://lccn.loc.gov/2023043834

Typeset by Hong Kong FIVE Workshop, Hong Kong
Print production managed by Jellyfish
Printed and bound by CPI Group (UK) Ltd, Croydon CR0 4YY

CONTENTS

The most important aspect of wellbeing is that it's personal; what works for me will not work for you necessarily. We all have different needs, and so any 'wellbeing expert' who claims to know exactly what you need will undoubtedly be wrong. Well-meaning applications and solutions can and do exacerbate stress if we do not create space for them. The biggest cause of stress in the workplace is workload and what do we do to fix this? We give people more tasks to do, more webinars, more apps, more fruit bowls. Seems sensible and logical.

Nowadays, we have an abundance of companies, individuals and 'experts' offering well-intended wellbeing solutions/advice. Even though the advice is often meant with good intention it fails to recognize that what works for one person does not work for another. As Mary Schmich said, 'Advice is a form of nostalgia. Dispensing it is a way of fishing the past from the disposal, wiping it off, painting over the ugly parts and recycling it for more than it's worth.'[1]

I am not a grumpy old man (not totally anyway), I simply suggest that we take all advice with a pinch of salt and consider what it means for us as individuals. If you're not sure what to do, ask yourself, 'What was the last thing that brought me joy?' (a deeper and less fleeting sense of happiness) and create space for some of that today. Of course, ignore all of this, as this is my advice about advice.

Mary Schmich, who I quoted above, opens her famous university address – 'Wear Sunscreen' – with, 'My advice has no basis more reliable than my own meandering experience,' Which I quite like. You and me both, Mary. Her address was adapted into the famous song by Baz Luhrmann, 'Everybody's Free (To Wear Sunscreen)'. I will come back to Mary's speech quite a few times throughout this book.

What works for one from a wellbeing perspective will not necessarily work for another. It is this author's hope that you take a lot from this book (as I have done over the past three years of writing it); there will be bits that resonate with you and there will also be bits that you think are nonsense and that is fine. As I said, what works for one does not necessarily work for another. This is why there are 52 different chapters, each containing a different wellbeing-based topic. I have combined the latest academic, cutting-edge thinking and what I have learned over the years to create what I hope are 52 practical/pragmatic chapters to make some lasting changes in your life. There is nothing that frustrates me more than 'wellbeing experts' who tell stories and leave you with nothing at the end: 'OK, now what?' This is not that book – it's as practical as it gets.

Although I can't change your workplace with this book – the workaholic culture, your bad manager or the sheer number of meetings you have to attend – I would if I could. It is my hope that by adopting a few of the tips from a few chapters in this book your perspective on workplace wellbeing will change. I hope that when you finish this book you will have adopted a flexibly non-negotiable attitude to your wellbeing and that you will ruthlessly prioritize what you need to be your best self each and every day. You are your priority. Forget work–life balance. It's just life, and while work is one part of it, it shouldn't be your first priority. You are your priority – don't worry, we'll come back to this later.

We seem to have confused ourselves in the modern workplace regarding what wellbeing actually is. Time for a reset: it is not an employer's responsibility to improve staff happiness at work. Let me repeat that: *it is not an employer's responsibility to improve staff happiness at work.*

OK, so if it's not bikes, bananas and one-off events, what is wellbeing at work then? According to the Gallup State of the Global Workplace report from 2023, it is:

- psychological safety – cultures where employees feel secure, like they belong and have the freedom to bring their own perspectives;
- flexibility – there is no one size fits all and we should focus on geographic, temporal and modal flexibility where possible;
- a focus on outcomes over hours – unless you're on an assembly line, the amount of time you work has not been shown to link to outputs and more does not equal more;
- increased autonomy – heightened autonomy improves engagement without compromising performance.[2]

Sounds good to me.

The largest study of wellbeing at work ever, conducted by Indeed and Forrester, actually asked people what they 'think' positively affects wellbeing and here is what people said (in order): fair pay, flexibility, inclusion, achievement, appreciation, belonging, support, trust, learning, manager support, feeling energized.[3] No surprises there.

But, as the report found, the order of what actually drives wellbeing is: feeling energized, belonging, trust, achievement, fair pay, inclusion, manager support, support, flexibility, appreciation, learning. Interesting, right? We think compensation will be top and it is fifth.

There is a reason Google prioritizes psychological safety as its number one priority for employees. Belonging is key, yet it is so quickly overlooked in the digital world. Most organizations with 'knowledge or digital' workers are trying and failing to find answers to the hybrid paradox. This is a term that Satya Nadella, the CEO of Microsoft, coined, finding that Microsoft employees want to keep their increased flexibility (>70 per cent), while they crave more in-person connection (>65 per cent).[4] This is perhaps one of the great organizational challenges of our time. We are plugged in like interfaces on machines, with four spare minutes per day, grinding out widgets: 'beep, boop, morp, zeep'. Are you feeling energized after a day of back-to-back calls?

Unsurprisingly, we are not especially happy about it. Especially in the UK, where according to Gallup, 90 per cent of us are disengaged at work.[5] Organizations that get the balance of flexibility and connection right will win the so-called 'war for talent'; they will keep their best and attract the rest.

Over the years, working with various organizations and governments around the world, I have found that I have been able to have a greater effect on wellbeing by not saying the word – the paradox of wellbeing. Paradoxes are like buses; you will wait all day for one and then two come along in short succession. The more you say the word wellbeing, the less likely it is to appear. I do see the irony, given the title of the book. When wellbeing has been my sole purpose, I have been limited in my scope and had to stick to one-off events, webinars and workshops. Plastering over symptoms of a problem. Now and again, my muzzle was removed and I was rolled out at certain times of the year for X day or Y week. Like Hannibal Lecter, I had to promise not to bite anyone or mention workloads. Did someone say Chianti?

We of course need these days, events and webinars for awareness; but for prevention, that's another matter entirely. Do we want to wait until someone is suffering to step in, or reduce the likelihood it will happen in the first place? Wellbeing at work is not a focus area, it's an outcome and it's my hope that instead of events on certain days of the year, we will begin to see more and more future-thinking organizations adopting four-day work weeks, unlimited paid leave, flexible hybrid policies, matched parental leave, etc. However, this is a topic for another book. I'm here to help *you*.

So, while it may not be an organization's responsibility to improve happiness, it is their responsibility not to worsen it. Fewer webinars and solutions; rather, a little bit of space, time, autonomy, flexibility and a sense of psychological safety will do perfectly. Thanks.

What you do with that space as an individual; well, that is up to you. I'm not going to tell you what to do.

If I were to ask you whether or not you felt stressed yesterday, what would you say? Take a second and think about it…

The Gallup Global Negative Experience Index, which measures stress as well as pain, worry, sadness and anger around the world, indicates that global unhappiness has risen by 37.5 per cent since 2010.[6] This paints a pretty bleak picture and you only have to ask those around you to get the feeling for yourself. Ask anyone how they feel and you will often hear: 'slammed, manic, back-to-back, drowning', etc.

Things have changed a lot for me too since 2010, as they have for all of us. Back in 2010, I was a trainee electrician two years into my apprenticeship; there were probably not any TED talks or books on the horizon for this version of Ryan Hopkins. Every weekend I played rugby and I loved it; it was who I was, my identity. One Saturday in January I went to play, not knowing that my life would never be the same again.

It was raining, the pitch was soaking, puddles everywhere. About halfway through the game, I took the ball into contact and was tackled. Nothing untoward about that. What was not good though, was that I was on the floor and my foot was still stuck in the ground. You know one of those horrible breaks, when a foot is facing the wrong way? Yeah, one of those. I was taken to hospital, where I was told that there was no pulse in my foot and they would have to pop it back in immediately, otherwise there was a chance I would lose my foot. I took a few big deep breaths on the gas and air, trying to get as high as possible for what was about to happen. 3, 2, 1… crunch. What they did not know at this time was that my leg was also broken. Apparently I screamed and then passed out. I do not remember this. Needless to say, the recovery was long.

I was wheelchair bound for the best part of a year, needing multiple operations. I was unable to work, putting an end to my career as an electrician; I was unable to play rugby; I put on a lot of weight; I was in debt; I had no qualifications; I had no prospects; I was truly and utterly miserable and I did not know what to do. I went to speak to my GP and he prescribed me a course of antidepressants. Not too long after this, on one of my regular wheelchair rides around the block, I could see myself as clear as day hanging from the trees in the woods. I stared and I stared at what I saw, it was as real as the hand in front of my face is now. It was then I made plans to take my own life and if it were not for the love and affection of my mum, I would not be here today.

However, back in 2010 it was not just me that was suffering – 66 people in every 1,000 in the UK were taking antidepressants. This being a fraction of the total number of people who were suffering at this time.[7]

After the most difficult year of my life, I got myself a job in a bank and on the surface it looked like I was doing great. I was one of the best salespeople in the country and as I gained the ability to walk again, I began to lose weight. A lot of weight. It was falling off me, but not in a healthy way. It was falling off as I had developed bulimia. I never told anyone, until the point that I nearly ended up in hospital. It was something I never thought a big rugby player like me could or would get. I hid it away, refusing to fully acknowledge it, fearing the judgement and shame that I believed would accompany it. After a year of struggling on my own, I told my mum and only because I had to. I was so calorie restricted (eating strictly chicken, broccoli, the water it was cooked in and chewing gum) at this point that I was struggling to speak and I was sent home from work. She sat me down, knowing something was wrong, and we shared a slice of cake together. Again, Mum to the rescue. This is not how everyone takes their first step on the journey of recovery, but it was how I took mine.

This was 2013, when things were not getting better for me, nor were they for a lot of other people. At this time, we now had 84 people per 1,000 on antidepressants in the UK, a 27 per cent increase since 2010.[8]

A few years later came 2016, the year of Brexit, Trump and Pokémon Go (at least we had that).

I finally got myself to university – I must have been the wildcard entry. I was getting good grades, playing rugby again. I was a big strong man; I worked as a bouncer and pulled double-decker buses for fun – I am still Hastings Bus Pull Champion, as the event was cancelled after 2014 due to health and safety concerns. On the surface, once again I appeared to be confident, to have it all together. Under the surface was another matter entirely. I was so anxious that every time I left my front door I felt like I was going to wet myself. If I had to travel I would wear an adult diaper as I was so concerned. It was a truly miserable period of my life. I was 105kg of anxious muscle.

In 2016, I was still struggling and so were a lot of people. In the UK in 2016, we had 101 out of 1,000 on antidepressants, a 53 per cent increase since we started our journey in 2010.[9]

Flash forward to 2022. Queen Elizabeth passed away, Russia invaded Ukraine and Elon Musk took over Twitter. I think 2022 gives 2016 a real run for its money. We now have 112 out of 1,000 on antidepressants – 11 per cent of the population, a 70 per cent increase since 2010.[10] This is one fraction of the people struggling – in 2020/21, 24 per cent of people in the UK were reporting some signs/evidence of anxiety or depression.[11] Oh, and compared to when we started our story in 2010, we are now spending 1,000 per cent more time on our screens.[12]

Does the 70 per cent increase in antidepressant usage signify a 70 per cent increase in depression? No, not necessarily. In 2010, 18 per cent of the UK were showing signs of anxiety/depression: in 2020/21 this was 24 per cent – a 33 per cent increase.[13] There was no data for 2022/23 available at the time of writing this book. This could mean that the use of antidepressants is being de-stigmatized and attitudes are changing. Regardless of the reason, the number of people suffering/struggling is increasing and things are not getting better from a mental health perspective.

We often see wellbeing as something added, something that is addressed reactively when we have a problem, rather than something we proactively create space for every day.

You could have offered me the world's best solution or application when I was at my lowest and I would not have wanted it, or been in the headspace to even consider using it. I just needed the love and affection of the people I care about. Well-meaning solutions, platforms, ideas and plans can actually stress us out further unless we create space.

There are 2,387 per cent more apps on the app store than in 2010,[14] with 350,000 of them being health apps,[15] and as we have discussed, things have never been worse. Some of these apps and solutions can legitimately change your life, but unless we change the system/organization to create some space, they will not get the chance to make a difference. There is no silver bullet.

I came to realize over the past 13 years, as I pieced myself back together again and again, that wellbeing is no small thing, but made up of small things. Wellbeing is completely individual and what works for one does not and will not work for another. In essence, what I learned is that big doors swing on little hinges.

Over the last 13 years, I have pretty much done every job there is to do, from sexual health adviser, headmaster of a school in Italy, bouncer, cocktail bar manager in Spain to starting a hostel business in Ecuador.

Think of a job. Yes, I've done that.

Think of another one. I haven't done that, I'm not that mad.

I spent years trying to work out what I wanted to do and when I finally figured it out, I tried my utmost to be someone else to fit in. I am fundamentally flawed, broken, messed up and surely it was only a matter of time until someone found out. Everyone else seems to have got it all together. Why am I so messed up? But I learned something pretty amazing and I want to share it with you: there is nothing wrong with me and there is definitely nothing wrong with you.

Six years ago, I started to share my story at the odd work event. One piece of my story at a time, as I began to take my masks off and felt comfortable. Each time I shared, I found out that there were 5, 10, 20 people like me. Three years ago, I decided to go one step further and started sharing my story on social media and I found out that there were 100, 1,000, even 1,000,000 people just like me.

Over the years in conversations around making positive wellbeing change, I found that wellbeing is either in complete crisis, or so 'woo woo' that it engages absolutely no one... you can't meditate your way out of a 14-hour day.

As I said earlier, big doors swing on little hinges and wellbeing is no small thing but made up of small things. James Clear's formula from *Atomic Habits*[16] is perfect for this, and I have added just one word:

Small, smart wellbeing choices, with consistency over time = a radical difference.

Can you guess which word I added? James also shares that if you improve by 1 per cent per day, you are 3,778 per cent better at the end of the year with compound interest.

This got me thinking, what is something we do each day regularly, that we could attach positive habits to?

Something we do eight times every day.

If you think you don't go to the toilet eight times every day, count tomorrow. You will be surprised. I was.

If we did 10 push-ups each time we washed our hands, we would do 29,200 this year; what about a couple of big deep breaths, think how much calmer you would feel; or even saying something nice to yourself in the mirror: 'You're doing good, you're not as terrible as you think you are.'

You are basically a house plant with more complicated emotions; you often just need a bit more sunshine and water.

This is where the concept of 'toilet break wellbeing' was born. I started with a few selfie videos in the bathroom, thinking to myself, 'this is where your career ends'. I said on day one that Toilet Break Wellbeing would be a book; it has since transformed into the book you are currently reading. Thank goodness. That was just the start, I now have a ring light set up in my bathroom and I have to warn friends and family before they use the bathroom to let them know there is not some dodgy OnlyFans content going on.

I intended on removing the seriousness around the subject, making it more fun, normalizing conversations around mental health by sharing my story and highlighting the impact of small, smart wellbeing decisions with consistency over time. One flush at a time. Also, partly in homage to the fact that for all of 2016–17 I felt like I was going to wet myself as soon as I left the front door and all I wanted was a toilet.

Time to flush and flourish.

Since embarking on my global journey on the commode, I have been made redundant twice; posted over 1,500 times across platforms; engaged millions of people in the betterment of wellbeing and I am now engaging 250,000 people per week. I've spoken at Amazon, Microsoft, The Economist, governments, delivered a TEDx talk, been recognized as Global Emerging Wellbeing Leader of the Year, been selected as a LinkedIn Top Voice and my team and I help organizations all around the world to develop wellbeing strategies that actually work, instead of the nonsense and noise we normally see. This is just the start, too; I aim to engage 1 billion people in the betterment of wellbeing.

Now, we are going to travel forward in time: it is 2034, David Beckham has just become Prime Minister in the UK. He is addressing the nation and has shared with us all that there is a global banana shortage and those that remain are worth more than bitcoin – which is now the global currency. But that is not the headline we are bothered about. He has also shared that (if we carry on as we are) we will have 204 people out of 1,000 on antidepressants and more than one in three people in the UK will be showing evidence of depression/anxiety. But I don't think that is going to happen and this is why.

Firstly, we are going to adopt an ever-increasing attitude of healthishness – being selfish with our health; it is really the least selfish thing we can do. We are going to ruthlessly prioritize the things that we need to be our best selves every day.

What brought me the most joy for years was blocking out my calendar for lunch, going for a walk and giving my nan a call. I started doing this during the pandemic for her, as she lived alone, but I carried on for three years for me. She passed away unexpectedly in May 2023 while I was writing this book and I will never get the chance to speak to her again and hear the words 'Hello sweetheart'. *You will see her mentioned throughout this book – she was a huge part of my life. Love you Red.*

I'll say it again: forget work–life balance; make space and time for the things that make you your best self and prioritize the hell out of them – these are your non-negotiables.

As the great Ru Paul says: 'If you don't love yourself, how the hell you gonna love anyone else?'

Secondly, we are going to continue to normalize conversations around mental health. Sure you have been through it, but you are still here. You are still here and you are still fighting. There is no tougher battle than the one you will fight in your own head. Trust me, I see you. It does not matter whether you share your story from a chair, a stool, the back of a horse or even your own toilet – all that matters is that you share your story, because helping one person may not change the world, but it may change the world for that one person.

So, now it is 2034 and Prime Minister Beckham has just shared the news that depression and anxiety have dropped again and we are now at pre-2010 levels.

As I mentioned, there is no silver bullet with regard to wellbeing; it is something we create space for every single day. Now we're going to explore 52 different subjects that will enable you to better prioritize and improve your wellbeing year-round. Not even James from HR will be able to ruin your day. Let's go!

Do you move more when you are in the office or when you are at home? What about Monday to Friday compared to the weekend?

Picture it in your mind's eye: it's Sunday afternoon, after a busy-ish Saturday full of chores and life admin and you go for a long walk somewhere green, you're wrapped up, hat and gloves on – warm and toasty. It's one of those crisp but sunny winter days; you find a nice country pub somewhere and stop in for a roast dinner. Beautiful. When you arrive home, you feel refreshed if not a little sluggish from the extra three Yorkshire puddings (for any international readers, this is a delicious particularly British carb overload consumed on Sundays) and whack on some crap television. You know those days. They are the best days. This was quintessentially a British Sunday, but you understand what I'm getting at. Regardless of where you reside, we all seem to forget how movement makes us feel when we wake up on Monday morning. Time to plug in again and then repeat Tuesday through Friday.

Most of us struggle to find time to engage in regular exercise, especially when we are busy with work and other life commitments. This is particularly true for those of us who are fortunate enough to have the opportunity to work from home or hybrid, where the longest walk is from the desk in the corner of our bedroom to the fridge. We sit for eight or more hours, hunched over our desks, oh the joy. As a result, it becomes almost impossible to meet the recommended 10,000 steps per day. I spoke to a friend the other day, who said they had a good day when they almost hit 1,000. No wonder that over 20 million people in the UK (around a third of the population) live with a musculoskeletal (MSK) condition, such as arthritis and lower back pain.[17] Physios worldwide rub their hands in tandem like an army of Montgomery Burnses from the Simpsons: '*excellent*'.

It is important to note here that some of us are unable to walk; the most important thing is to move, however you can, in your own way.

When I pack my lunch box, iron a shirt and head into the office (with marmalade sandwiches, just like Paddington Bear), I will hit 10,000+ steps without thinking. I walk to the gym, from the gym to the office, around the office all day from meeting to meeting – all the while necking lattes like they're going out of fashion – back to the tube station and walk/dawdle back from there while chatting to my mum on the phone.

As someone who is temporally challenged (like you, I have a shed load of meetings and am time poor), I understand the struggle of trying to maintain an active routine amidst a busy work schedule. If I do not plan and prioritize it, it will not happen. It's that simple. So, what do we do about it?

The first step to incorporating physical activity into your daily routine is to make time for it, to plan it in – sounds awfully simple, but do you do it? If we wait or rely on our trusty willpower, post a nine-hour work day, what is going to win – a gym session or a couple of cookies dunked into a nice cup of milk and a Netflix marathon? I hear from a lot of friends, family and colleagues, 'Oh, Ryan, I would love to, I just don't have enough time to exercise or get out for a walk.' Excuses, excuses. The reality is that we make time for the things that are important to us and if we want to live a long, healthy and happy life, this is something we all need to do. It does not even have to be a walk, but you can move in some way, shape or form. All that matters is that we just do a little bit of physical activity most days:

Tip 1: Schedule it into your diary like you would a doctor's appointment. Hopefully by scheduling and prioritizing your walk, you will need less of them – doctor's appointments that is.

Tip 2: Block your calendar. Put on your Out Of Office. Let people who you work with know that you are stepping away for a walk (if you are able to, of course) and chances are those around you will start to do the same. Try and align with your team if you can. By prioritizing yourself and health, you will inspire others to do the same.

Tip 3: Walk and talk. This is a classic two birds, one stone scenario: walk and talk meetings. Let people know that your meeting will be a walking one and they can get out, too. This tends to work better if you are a listener rather than a talker (do not forget to mute yourself), and when it's thunderstorming in the UK, it's not conducive for productive meetings. Yes I have tried and failed. 'Sorry, could you repeat that?'

Tip 4: Scope/locate places of interest. I have found and plotted my favourite coffee shops and green spaces around my home and the office. I know that if I have 30 minutes, I need to select one of my 10–15-minute walk options and if I have 50 minutes, I can opt for one of my 20–25-minute options. I have pinned all of these places in maps on my phone, so I pop my hat on and head out, no time wasted on thinking where to go. Sometimes I go a bit wild and just walk and see where my feet take me. Yes, I'm a renegade and I know it.

Tip 5: Walk with the world's best. I am lucky enough to walk with Tim Ferris, Greg McKeown, Srinivas Rao, Seth Godin et al every day. No, these incredible humans do not live in South West London and join me for a walk. I wish. Rather I listen to their podcasts when I'm pounding the streets of Fulham. I love my walking time and always come back refreshed, having learned a thing or two. Sometimes, though, I will head out without my phone and walk more slowly around the park – it just depends how loud the traffic is in my head that day.

Walking also has the added benefit of burning calories, if you did not already know. This book will be full of blindingly obvious revelations. Walking for just 30 minutes can burn approximately 175 calories. Over the course of a year, this can add up to a significant amount of calories. How many do you reckon? Don't look down – try and work it out.

You're very naughty – I know you looked.

It's 63,875. Yep, that is a lot. This will result in a potential weight loss of over 18 pounds in a year. This is a great way to achieve your fitness goals without having to spend hours at the gym, engaging in the latest fitness trend, trying the latest diet or spending hundreds on an elliptical trainer that turns into a clothes dryer within three weeks.

Our daily walks not only have a positive impact on our physical health, but also benefit our mental health massively. Countless studies over the years have shown that physical activity helps to reduce stress, improve cognitive function and boost our overall mood. Just a 30-minute walk each day can significantly improve your mental wellbeing, leaving you feeling more focused and energized. What is not to like? Given how much I am advocating for taking a stroll, I actually never 'walked' prior to the pandemic. However, now I could not imagine going a day without stepping outside for a little stomp.

By allocating just 30 minutes each day for a walk or some other form of physical activity, you will significantly improve your physical and mental health. Plus, you could potentially fit into those old trousers that have been hiding in the back of the cupboard for longer than you care to think about. Maybe you can't get out for as long as you would like, but the most important thing is that you get out and move a little. Little and often is key.

Time to lace up those trainers and get outside!

02
REDUCING THE NOISE

Every single day we are bombarded with information from the moment we peel ourselves out of bed to the moment we shut our eyes. With the rise of technology and the internet, it's easier than ever to stay connected to the world around us. The little supercomputer in your pocket has over 100,000 times the processing power of the computer that landed man on the moon 50 years ago, so no wonder we cannot peel ourselves away. Never have information, content, the latest goings on been so readily available. However, with this constant flow of information comes a new challenge: the sheer amount of it that we receive. From email notifications to social media alerts, it can feel like we are always 'on' and never truly able to disconnect.

I just checked my phone to see what the last notification was – apparently my contents insurance is expiring in a couple of months. Helpful, yes. But did I need a notification, an email and a text message to remind me?

The average person now receives 63.5 notifications per day, according to *Wired*.[18] Now that is a lot of interruptions and distractions! It is no wonder we often feel overwhelmed and stressed. We have become conditioned to constantly check our phones, just in case we have missed something important – 'ah, ASOS is having a sale'. We just cannot help but peek into the digital cookie jar – which the average US citizen does, glancing at their phones 352 times per day.[19] If we did anything else 352 times per day, we would say we had a problem, right? Try not to check your phone for an hour. See how you get on. You will feel the phantom twitch in your leg – that is a thing.

With the constant barrage of information, most of which is involuntary, it's more important than ever to remember that we are what we consume and this goes far beyond food and drink. Every notification we receive and interact with influences how we think and feel, whether we realize it or not. If you are plugged into the news cycle 24/7, how do you think that is going to make you feel? Good news doesn't make news. By taking back control of the notifications we receive, we can ensure that we are mostly only consuming information that is truly beneficial to us or going to uplift us.

So, what can we do to reduce the noise and take back control? Who knows, maybe we could even focus for 10 whole seconds. Take that goldfish! Here are a few tips:

Tip 1: Delete it. We often download apps on a whim, without really thinking about whether we need them or not, and accept all notifications: 'Join the mailing list for 5 per cent off your next cupcake' – 'Yes please, take my details.' Take a look at your phone and ask yourself, 'Do I really need apps for all 17 coffee shops I have visited recently?' If the answer is no, then delete the apps and all the others you don't need and/or use. This will not only free up space on your phone, but it will also reduce the number of notifications you receive, freeing up some well-needed mental space.

Tip 2: Social media notifications. We are all aware that social media can be a major source of distraction; anyone who has tried and failed to just spend two minutes on

TikTok will agree (speaking from first-hand experience). We are constantly receiving notifications about new likes, comments and messages. Time to reduce this noise, time to turn off all social media notifications. This will allow you to check in on your own terms, rather than constantly being bombarded with updates about stuff you could not care less about.

Tip 3: Do not disturb. Most smartphones have a 'do not disturb' feature that allows you to temporarily silence all notifications. Limit the window by which you are exposed to notifications; set up a routine so that your phone automatically goes into 'do not disturb' mode during certain hours of the day.

Tip 4: Mute all work notifications. Do you really need to be double pinged every time you receive a work email or message? Probably not. Mute all work notifications on your phone – that's what your laptop is for.

Tip 5: Nuclear option. Switch off all notifications except calls on your phone. No alerts, no banners, no nothing. I have done this and it works for me. I check when I want to check, not the other way around, much to the chagrin of my friends I'm chatting to on WhatsApp.

Tip 6: Go on holiday. Want peace and quiet? Simple, put your phone in airplane mode.

Tip 7: Leave it behind. Sometimes the best way to reduce the noise is to simply leave it behind. Yes, it does feel weird at first, but you get used to it. If you are spending quality time with family and friends, leaving your phone at home can be quite liberating. Don't get lost, though.

By implementing these tips, we can take back control of the sheer number of notifications we receive on a daily basis and reduce the noise in our lives. Remember, your phone works for you, not the other way around.

Time to take back control!

Do you have a friend who seems to always find something to complain about? They could find a £5 note and be annoyed it wasn't a £20. You ask them how they are, and you will get a deep sigh and some form of moan. We all have at least one person like this in our lives. If you cannot think who this is, well... It is essential to remember that nothing is inherently good or bad; it's our perception that labels it as such, according to the stoics, anyway. If we constantly look for things to be annoyed about, we will undoubtedly find them. Of course, some things are genuinely terrible, and it's reasonable to feel annoyed or upset about them. However, most things are not as terrible as we make them out to be.

For example, if your train is delayed, are you annoyed or is it just a part of daily life? Maybe it's an opportunity to send a voice note to a loved one, wishing them a good day and hoping they make it to work without delay. In addition, it's a chance to enjoy and share a profound sense of schadenfreude at your own expense. Schadenfreude – the German word that means experiencing pleasure, joy or self-satisfaction from learning of or witnessing the troubles, failures or humiliation of another. Who doesn't like a bit of schadenfreude?

This is brought to life perfectly by the burnt toast theory. If you burn your toast in the morning, the time you spend making more toast may have saved you from a car accident.

Or it might make you late to a meeting but there's a chance that you will meet someone on the way that becomes special in your life. A reminder that the universe protects you.

So, who is up for a sunnier disposition in just 28 days? With only the cost of a single elastic band.

Tip 1: The language audit. You are going to kick off your journey to a sunnier disposition by paying attention to how you answer when people ask how you are or how your day is going. Be particularly conscious of your response to 'negative' moments. Write your answers down and capture them in notes on your phone. You might be surprised by how negative your language is. Be honest with yourself.

Tip 2: Elastic band. Find and put an elastic band on your wrist. Every time you complain, you take it off and switch it over on to your other wrist. Repeat until the band has stayed put for 28 days. When you complain, you start at day one again. No ifs, no buts, no maybes.

What is a complaint anyway? Complaining is defined as 'describing an event or person negatively without indicating next steps to fix the problem'. We all need to blow off steam sometimes, but unless you're going to do something about it, is complaining helping you, your friend or the situation?

When I tried this for myself, I failed regularly in the first few days, catching myself and having to switch the band. I found myself back at day one fairly frequently. I did not think I complained much until I put the band on. However, I was quite surprised at how often I would start to moan about this or that, look down and think, 'bloody hell I've done it again'. It happened more than 20 times before I finally started to get the hang of it and I was on a bit of a spree…

But then a real test of my journey to a sunnier disposition reared its head. I have been quite busy recently, and I thought to myself, 'I would love a lockdown weekend'. I wanted a quiet weekend, simply punctuated by walks and takeaways. I wished I was not so busy. Well, I got what I wished for, but not in the way I wanted. I caught the flu and spent the entire weekend in bed or under a duvet on the couch. All my plans were cancelled. I felt sorry for myself and wanted to complain, but then I looked at my wrist. I thought to myself, 'unless I'm going to do anything about it, will moaning help me?'. Nope. So, I shifted my focus onto the fact that I got what I wished for. I ordered more sushi than one person can eat, drank litres of tea and rolled myself into a human burrito. 'Yes, Netflix, I am still watching.'

By making small changes to my language and focusing on the positive, I was able to shift my perspective and enjoy my weekend. It's not easy, but with a little effort, we can put on our rose-tinted glasses and find a positive, because what is the alternative?

Fix the words, and you fix the thoughts.

Stick on the TV or open the news app on your phone and you will find headline after headline of chaos, disaster and mayhem. Fears, fires and fake news dominate our screens and consequently our attention (as we discussed in Chapter 2). It's no wonder that doom scrolling – the act of endlessly scrolling through negative news – is directly linked to increased levels of stress and anxiety.[20] We are addicted to the 24-hour news cycle, believing that we need to stay informed about everything happening in the world. But at what cost? And do we need to be?

The news is not so much about reporting the facts, but about sensationalizing and dramatizing events and stories to capture our attention. We do live in an attention economy after all, wherein your eyeballs are highly sought-after commodities. In the battle to win eyeballs around the globe, the headline 'Good news, all is well in the world' does not work half as well as murder, war, death, panic, pandemic. Despite common belief, Matt Ridley, the author of *The Rational Optimist*, shares that

> We are living through the greatest improvement in human living standards in history. Extreme poverty has fallen below 10 per cent of the world's population for the first time. It was 60 per cent when I was born. Global inequality has been plunging as Africa and Asia experience faster economic growth than Europe and North America; child mortality has fallen to

record low levels; famine virtually went extinct; malaria, polio and heart disease are all in decline.[21]

That is boring, though.

Those pesky immigrants are coming, and not only are they stealing your jobs, but they are coming here to not work and to commit crime. Beware, be scared, tell people and read more. Such narratives create fear and anger, driving a wedge between communities and causing unnecessary tension. Oh, but it does generate views, clicks and shares. Who wants community anyway?

It's easy to fall into the trap of believing that we need to stay up to date with every current event, every single development, but the reality is that most news stories have little impact on our daily lives. We need to be particularly mindful of the impact of 'news' on our mental health. Like anything, consuming too much negative news is not good for us and can lead to feelings of anxiety, depression and hopelessness. It can also lead to a distorted view of the world, making us believe that everything is negative and that the world is a dangerous place – which of course it is sometimes. But, as Matt Ridley says, it is the best it has ever been.

But what about the good news? Why is it that positive stories rarely make the headlines? In fact, can you remember a time when you saw a positive headline? It's time to shift the dial to positive and crank it to 10. We have the option to focus on positive, uplifting stories that inspire and encourage us: a podcast, book, chat with a friend or even learn something that doesn't want to make you cry. They are all great alternatives.

Personally, I've deleted all news apps on my phone (except the *Financial Times*, which I do peruse on the tube on the way to work) and don't watch or listen to the news at home.

I used to know if a news story was particularly important if my nan told me about it during our lunchtime chats.

Of course, it is important to stay informed, but we need to do it in a way that doesn't compromise our happiness and sanity. If you are ready to limit/reduce your news intake, here are a few tips on how to stay informed, just without all the negativity (if you don't have a nan available every day for the daily update):

Tip 1: You know this one, the nuclear option. Delete the apps, or you can delete all but one like I have, there is simply no need for multiple.

Tip 2: Choose your news sources carefully. When you do engage, make sure to use reputable sources and try to avoid sources that sensationalize events for clickbait or who promote a particular agenda.

Tip 3: Breaking the news cycle. Set aside specific times of the day to check the news; no need to have it up on your browser all the time. And switch those notifications off.

Tip 4: Detox time. If you are feeling particularly overwhelmed or anxious by what's going on in the world (we all do sometimes), take a break from the news for a few days, a week, a month…

Tip 5: Good news. Seek out stories that inspire and encourage you. There is a lot of uplifting content/news out there if you know where to look

We have the power to choose how, where, when we stay in touch with coming and goings on in the world. Time to take control of our news intake and make positive, informed choices about how we engage with the world around us, because remember you are what you consume.

Breaking news does not have to break us.

AND BREATHE

Do you feel like you are constantly staring at one screen or another? Between laptops, phones, TVs, most of us spend the vast majority of our waking lives in front of one. I am currently writing this book in a coffee shop on my iPad and I will head back home to relax and watch the Scotland vs France rugby game on TV in the Six Nations. I just can't wait until the neural link is developed and launched and I can watch Netflix in my sleep... What happened to those Google glasses, too? I have to walk home soon and I'm going to have to look at a tree or something. Ugh.

The average adult spends just over seven hours looking at a screen every day (and I would say this is a conservative figure).[22] The very rare moment that we find ourselves without a screen, we will be reminiscing, reflecting, planning or forecasting; essentially, doing anything apart from being present. We only exist in the present moment, which is why it's called the present – it is a gift. The past is history and the future is a mystery.

If you find yourself constantly distracted, switched on, plugged in, overwhelmed, etc, which you do, one solution you could consider is meditation and/or breath work. The word meditation can invoke a strange response and will either seem very intimidating to those who have never done it, or just a bit 'woo woo' and 'soft'. The people who feel this way are often the ones who need it the most. I worked on building sites for years in a previous life and (prepare yourself for a sweeping generalization) they are not the 'sort' of people who will go to yoga or a meditation class. However, they do have multiple cups of tea (often in silence) – like, a lot.

So, here are two simple tips for incorporating mindfulness and breath work into your daily routine:

Tip 1: A mindful cuppa. Take a moment to make yourself a cup of tea or coffee (or whatever your preferred drink is) and enjoy it without any screens. Find a quiet spot outside or near a window, and simply focus on the drink – the flavour, the smell, the heat of it. If your mind starts to wander, gently bring it back to the drink. Not only will you be re-caffeinated, but you'll also feel rejuvenated – it's a win–win.

Tip 2: Box breathing. In just 16 seconds, you can lower your blood pressure, decrease cortisol (the stress hormone), ease panic and worry, and reduce feelings of overwhelm and stress, creating a sense of focus and calmness. It's a simple practice that anyone can do, no matter how busy you are. I like to do three rounds before a big presentation.

Here is how to do it: Sit upright in a chair with your feet on the floor with your back supported. Close your eyes and place your hand on your stomach. Breathe deeply and focus on the rise and fall of your belly:

Step 1: Breathe in slowly through your nose, counting to 4–6. Feel the air enter your lungs.

Step 2: Hold your breath for 4–6 seconds. Avoid inhaling or exhaling during this time.

Step 3: Slowly exhale through your mouth for 4–6 seconds.

Step 4: Repeat steps 1 to 3 until you feel calm and focused.

Incorporating mindfulness and/or breath work into your daily routine does not have to be complicated or time consuming. By simply taking a few minutes each day to focus on your breath or enjoy a cup of tea, you can de-stress and prepare yourself for whatever the world has to throw at you.

Remember, we live one breath at a time.

It's no secret that many of us prioritize work over wellbeing. It's not even up for debate. Work first, life second, end of. Even before the pandemic, a third of UK workers admitted to eating at their desk and the majority of the other two-thirds would drop lunch at the drop of a hat if work demanded it.[23] The shift to more digital ways of working have only exacerbated this problem, with 67 per cent of those working remotely feeling pressured to be available at all hours of the day, even when sick.[24]

This paints a pretty bleak and dystopian future; however, it's not all bad. According to the World Economic Forum, we now work from home for an average of 1.7 days per week.[25] This saves two hours of commuting per week: 40 per cent of this time is spent working, 34 per cent goes on leisure and 11 per cent on caregiving. This is literally alchemy with your most precious resource, your time. As damaging and difficult as the pandemic was and considering the desire to be constantly available, this is still a gift. A gift that enables a more equal share of the parenting responsibilities, improved opportunities for underrepresented demographics (making a geographically agnostic workplace), reduced pollution and expansion of personal freedoms – the list goes on.

So, there are challenges to the digitally connected workplace, but there are also immense opportunities that we are going to make the most of together. We are going to make appointments with ourselves and honour those appointments just as we would a work meeting or dentist's appointment. Take time for a cup of coffee, eat lunch away from your laptop, schedule a walk or gym session, and do not apologize for it. While it may be tempting to prioritize work over personal appointments, neglecting to take care of ourselves can and will lead to negative consequences in the long run. 'Oh, just one more email won't hurt…' You are your priority and the sooner you realize that the happier, healthier and, conversely, more productive you will be. If you don't prioritize yourself, you won't be able to prioritize anything or anyone else.

One incredible leader I used to work with (shout out to Jess) always blocked out her lunch break on her calendar and if someone scheduled a meeting over it, she simply declined without feeling guilty or offering an explanation. But this is not a topic that just relates to work teams – we often say yes to things we don't actually want to do and drop personal appointments quicker than a hot pitta bread out of the toaster (which is widely known to be the hottest thing on planet Earth). As a self-proclaimed people pleaser, I used to say 'yeah' or 'maybe' to almost every offer, postponing/cancelling any self-care I had planned.

'Want to go and see that latest French feature film?' – You bet. Ever been woken up for snoring in a cinema? Nah, me neither.

'Want to go to a work event across the other side of London on a Monday night?' 100 per cent… until I realize that I need to catch five different trains home.

'Want to attend this lunch and learn?' Please do not get me started on lunch and learns. They should be stricken from the earth. It's either lunch or learn. If we are that time poor that we cannot eat lunch in peace, well then, we have bigger worries. Also, what is this dystopian hell where lunch and learns don't come with lunch? That's just 'learn instead of lunch'.

To start resetting, refreshing and reprioritizing your personal appointments, here are a few tips:

Tip 1: Book it in. If it's not in the calendar, it probably won't happen. Do not leave your self-care up to chance. Schedule it in, just as you would any other important meeting or appointment. I find that if I do not schedule and do certain things pre-work, then there is almost zero chance that I will do them after work.

Tip 2: Priorities. If you are not aware of what you need to do every day to be your best self, then how are you going to prioritize those activities? You need to understand what these things are and prioritize them ruthlessly (see Chapter 11, 'Non-negotiable wellbeing').

Tip 3: The magic two-letter word. When asked to do something, it's either 100 per cent yes or no. Saying 'maybe' or 'perhaps' only postpones the decision and leaves less time for self-care. Saying a polite 'no thanks' leaves space in your life for those personal appointments for self-care and other opportunities. Remember, a no now is a yes in the bank for later.

Tip 4: Tracking. A good friend of mine once told me, 'What gets measured, gets incentivized, gets improved.' It is so true. Write down your priorities and track whether they happen or not. Use a habit tracker to keep yourself accountable. I check in at the end of each day; it keeps me honest and helps me to reflect and learn from where I slip up. 'OK, so I didn't walk enough today, why was that?' Maybe it was the 13 video calls? Maybe.

Tip 5: Healthishness. Prioritizing your health is not selfish – in fact, it is the least selfish thing you can do. Adopt an attitude of 'healthishness' and take care of yourself first, so that you are better equipped to take care of others. Think of this attitude as your life jacket. When you put this on first, you'll be able to help those around you. Remember that if you neglect to put your life jacket on, then you are going to be unable to look after anything or anyone else as you will be splashing around and probably more likely to hinder than help.

Taking care of yourself is not a selfish act – far from it. By ruthlessly prioritizing your personal appointments, you will be better equipped to handle the demands of work and daily life and you will thrive in any environment you find yourself in.

07

THE WORLD'S GREATEST STRETCH

Musculoskeletal conditions affect 1.7 billion people world-wide, with one of the most prevalent issues being lower back pain.[26] Upper for me, but I have always been different. With more people working from home than ever and our lives becoming increasingly sedentary, many of us are experiencing discomfort and tension all the way from our heads and shoulders through our knees to our toes. If only there were one stretch that could help alleviate some of this pain...

Introducing the world's greatest stretch. This full-body stretch targets several muscle groups at once, alleviating tension in the lower back, upper back, glutes and hips, and can be done anywhere, at any time. So, put your phone down, step away from the emails and let us do this together. If you want to watch a video, there are plenty on YouTube to choose from.

To perform the world's greatest stretch, start by stepping forward with your right leg into a lunge, ensuring that your foot is flat on the floor (barefoot is better, but please do not take your shoes off in the office) and your knee is bent at a 90-degree angle. Place both of your hands flat on the floor inside your right leg and allow yourself to feel a slight stretch in your hips – 'oh yeah, that's the good stuff'. Noises encouraged.

Next, lift your right hand off the floor, bend your right elbow and let it fall towards your right foot. Reach your elbow towards your right foot as far as you can without rounding your back. Staying in the lunge position, rotate your whole upper body to the right, pressing through your left palm, and lift your right arm straight up to the ceiling. Look up at your arm, ensuring that your back is straight and your core is engaged. Now we're talking.

Twist again through the spine to return your right arm with your elbow still bent back to the ground in front of you. Finally, step back into a plank position and repeat the entire sequence on your left side. Remember to breathe deeply into the discomfort (which will be there) and hold each stretch for a few seconds to really get into it. Enjoy this time. This is your time; nothing and no one else matters right now.

By performing the world's greatest stretch regularly, you will begin to improve your flexibility, strengthen your core and alleviate the tension in your lower back and hips that builds up in us throughout the day. This stretch is particularly beneficial for those who sit for long periods during the day or suffer from tight hip flexors, as it can help to improve your posture and alleviate stiffness in your joints; it does for me anyway and I suffer with back pain daily. Perhaps more importantly, it's a bit of time for you to focus on you – no distractions, no commitments, just you making some 'ugghhhs and ahhhs'.

This is a fantastic stretch and perfect when you are short of time, but here are some additional tips for incorporating a bit more stretching into your day:

Tip 1: Couch to floor. Put a yoga mat in front of your TV. This way you can unwind, watch some *Below Deck*, listen to Captain Lee say 'Godddaaaammmmiiiiiitt' multiple times and stretch at the same time. Better than folding into the sofa for five hours.

Tip 2: Toilet stretch. Combine the stretching with another behaviour, e.g. each time you go to the toilet, reach for your toes. Not at the same time, of course. That might make a mess. You go to the toilet roughly eight times every day and if we do a little stretch each time, you will be surprised how quickly you will be touching those toes of yours.

It's common knowledge that stretching is a crucial part of maintaining good physical health, preventing injury, maintaining fitness, etc. Yet it is the element of physical training that is the first to be dropped, as it's not as exciting as whatever else it is you have to do today. Use the tips above and when you are short of time utilize the world's greatest stretch, as it targets multiple muscle groups simultaneously.

So why not give it a try today? Your body and mind will thank you for it!

08
SAY CHEESE

When was the last time you genuinely smiled? Not the polite smile you give to a stranger on the train or the fake smile you use for your building pass at work (has anyone ever taken a good one of those? I look like Nacho Libre in mine), but a true and heartfelt smile that makes your cheeks hurt. This smile deficiency seems to affect adults more than children... I would probably smile more too if I didn't have to pay taxes, deal with a bad back and could spend my days kicking leaves and jumping in puddles. It seems that somewhere along the way, through our formative years, we have lost our natural inclination to smile. What about the last time you laughed so much you shed a tear? Remember that?

But what if I told you that there are benefits to smiling that go beyond just looking happy and/or creeping out unsuspecting strangers on your morning commute? It turns out that smiling has real physiological effects on our body and mind. When we smile, our brains release dopamine, endorphins and serotonin, our feel-good hormones.[27] These hormones are responsible for reducing stress and anxiety, boosting our immune system and improving our overall mood (there are plenty more benefits, but you get it). Surprisingly, it has been shown that even fake smiles can produce these positive effects. Time to get those gnashers of yours out. If a new supplement were released to the market with all of these benefits, you would have ordered it already.

OK, here's where it gets really interesting – it's not just our own mind and body that benefit from smiling. Research suggests that when we see someone else smiling, our brains automatically begin to create the feel-good hormones, triggering the same positive response in ourselves. This is called emotional contagion, and it explains why seeing a happy, smiling face can lift our mood and make us feel more positive, while a frown and a scowl can do the opposite.

So, how can you incorporate more smiles into your daily life and benefit from those feel-good hormones?

Tip 1: Smile more. One simple solution is to make a conscious effort to smile more often, particularly when you don't feel like it. A study conducted at the University of Kansas found that smiling, even when we are not feeling at our most cheery, can actually boost our mood and reduce stress levels.[28] It's a bit like the old saying 'fake it till you make it'. By forcing a smile on ourselves, we can trick our brains into releasing those feel-good hormones, and eventually the smile becomes genuine. Wow, science.

Tip 2: Feedback loop of happiness. Another way to incorporate more smiles into your day is to make a real effort to smile at others. Whenever you meet someone new, make an effort to smile and greet them warmly, regardless of your mood. You never know how much a simple smile can mean to someone. It could be the first conversation they have had all day or perhaps you are the first person who has taken a second to check in. In an increasingly digital world, this can and does make all the difference. And for the Machiavellian among us, remember that when we smile at others, we often receive a smile in return, creating the positive feedback loop of feel-good hormones we discussed before.

Tip 3: Doorway smile. So, here is a little challenge for you: every time you walk into a room (even a digital room), smile broadly. You will feel silly at first, but I promise that it will soon become very normal, as will all the reciprocated smiles you receive in return. Remember, life is like a mirror – smile at it, and it smiles back at you.

Maybe you won't smile 400 times tomorrow, as you still have to go to work and have a three-hour finance call, but you can definitely do better than 20. As the Joker says, 'Why so serious?' It's time to commit to smile more; you will be amazed at the positive effects it has on your mood, your relationships and your overall outlook. As Mother Teresa once said, 'We shall never know all the good that a simple smile can do.' That could be a literary first – the Joker and Mother Teresa in one paragraph. Makes me smile thinking about it.

So, what are you waiting for? Say cheese!

09
BREAD ON THE HOOK

In today's world, we are bombarded with thousands of advertisements every day, each one trying to sell us something that promises to fill the voids in our lives. In the 1970s, the average person in the United States was exposed to about 500 ads per day, which seems like a lot – well, that is nothing compared to the present day. We are now exposed to over 5,000 ads today, almost one every 10 seconds that our eyes are open.[29] We are constantly told that happiness can be found through external means and that we need to consume more to achieve it. Happiness is attainable, you just have to pay XX amount for it. However, we all know deep down that material possessions only bring temporary relief and a fleeting sense of happiness.

So, what's the secret to unlocking this sense of joy? The answer is within ourselves – it's gratitude. Gratitude can be a powerful tool that can help us shift our focus from what we lack to what we have. It can make us appreciate the small things in life and cultivate a sense of contentment and joy. And the best part? It's completely free.

Here are two simple ways you can incorporate a bit more gratitude into your life and experience the benefits that come with it. These tips don't require any special skills, a lot of free time or even any resources; rather a willingness to cultivate a grateful mindset. So, let's get cracking.

Tip 1: Three things. One way to practise gratitude is to write down three things you are thankful for before you go to bed. These things can be as simple as having a roof over your head, a warm bed to sleep in, the delicious meal you had for dinner, a call with a loved one or a smile from a stranger on the train (someone else probably read this book and is on the previous chapter). It does not matter whether you had a bad day or a good day, there is always something to be grateful for – sometimes it may just take a bit longer before it comes to mind. By focusing on the positive aspects of our lives, we train our minds to see the positive, where perhaps we may have only focused on the negatives beforehand.

Tip 2: Paying it forward. Paying it forward is the act of doing something kind for someone without expecting anything in return. Not only does this benefit the person you are helping, but it triggers the release of those feel-good hormones we know and love. Just consider gift giving at Christmas, or any other religious holiday – do you prefer giving or receiving presents? You do not have to tell me. 'Ahhh, great, more socks.'

One way to pay it forward is to perform a random act of kindness. It can be something as simple as holding the door open for someone, offering to carry groceries for an elderly person or buying a coffee for the person behind you in line. I took my own advice and did this the other day.

I ordered my coffee and then turned around and asked what the lady behind me wanted. At first she was rather shocked at being accosted by the tattooed bald man at 7.50 am on a Tuesday, but it quickly turned into confusion and finally gratitude. Everyone in the coffee shop looked up and took notice of the commotion, and soon staff and customers alike were smiling. I left that coffee shop with a spring in my step and I felt immensely grateful all day. I said to the lady as I left, 'Pay it forward and do the same for someone else one day.' How can you pay it forward today?

You're still wondering what the title of this chapter means, aren't you? When buying a loaf of bread in a local bakery in Turkey, you can opt to pay for a second loaf, which the owner will hang on a hook outside. This is called Askida Ekmek. If a person in need comes by, they can ask if there is anything on the hook. If so, the bread is shared, hunger is satiated and community is built. When you choose to share your stories about your mental health, ask people how they are and role model good behaviours you are performing an equally generous act. Your courage and vulnerability are the bread on the hook and may be what someone in need is looking for. So ask yourself, how can you put some bread on the hook today?

In conclusion, gratitude is a powerful tool that can significantly improve our wellbeing and happiness. By practising gratitude and paying it forward, we can cultivate a positive mindset and make a positive impact on the world around us. So why not start today? Take a moment to reflect on the things you are grateful for and look for ways to spread kindness to those around you. You might be surprised at how much of a difference it can make in your life and the lives of others.

I've never met anyone who is not grateful for practising gratitude. What do you have to lose?

10
TOUCHING BASE

In today's fast-paced world, it can be easy to overlook the importance of human connection. You hardly have time to neck a cortado on the move to your next appointment, let alone sit down with someone to have a conversation. With the birth of the smartphone, creation of social media and messaging apps, we are more connected than ever before. Yet despite this, studies show that loneliness is becoming increasingly prevalent, particularly among young people. According to recent research, 61 per cent of young people aged 18–25 report that they feel lonely almost all the time.[30] This is the paradox of connection, which has only been exacerbated by the pandemic, as people were forced to isolate and distance themselves from others and many of us have little ventured out of the safety of our cocoons since.

It's easy to feel like we are alone in our loneliness, because that's what a feeling of loneliness is, right? However, the data shows that you are far from alone; in fact, you are in the majority by feeling alone. For me, there is a comforting solace in knowing that fact. As capable or even as solitary as we may view ourselves, no person is an island and we all need a support system to lean on when things get tough. That is where the importance of touching base with our loved ones comes in. It can be as simple as a quick message to let someone know that you are thinking of them, or a five-minute phone call while you are out on a walk.

These little acts of connection may only take a few seconds out of our day, but they could be the most important part of someone else's. A kind word or gesture can have a huge impact on someone's day. It can make them feel seen, heard and valued, even if just for a moment. This is exemplified by the fact that those with a 'work best friend' are twice as likely to feel satisfied at work and a third less likely to leave.[31] There is nothing like a well-timed GIF during a meeting to lighten the mood – my personal favourite is Homer Simpson moving backwards into the trees – 'Dohhh'.

During the pandemic, I made it a point to speak to my nan every day at lunch. It was a simple routine that we established early on in lockdown, and then continued on. I didn't realize how much it meant to me until my nan fell ill and was unable to speak for a few days. Those days without our daily calls felt empty and lonely. It was a stark reminder of how much I valued our connection, and how much it meant to both of us. As you know already, she passed away while I wrote this book. Call a loved one – you never know when they will no longer be around.

It's easy to assume that reaching out to someone else is all about making them feel good, a truly altruistic deed. You are just such a good person! But the truth is, it's just as important for our sense of wellbeing. Human connection is essential to our sense of belonging and purpose. Over 50,000 years ago, our ancestors who were expelled from the tribe would die of exposure or be eaten by an eager and hungry pack of lions. Exclusion and isolation from the tribe meant death and our neural chemistry has not evolved since then. Being isolated/disconnected is so much more than a rather unpleasant feeling; we will age faster, experience high levels of fatigue, have a weakened immune system and are 26 per cent more likely to die prematurely.[32] Damn.

So, the next time you are feeling overwhelmed, stressed or just a bit down, take a moment to reach out to someone that you care about. It doesn't have to be a long conversation or anything too onerous. A simple message or phone call can make all the difference in the world. And who knows, you might just make someone's day in the process. Here are a few practical tips for touching base more regularly:

Tip 1: Connection time. Whether it is a daily phone call or a weekly check-in, make it a priority to touch base with your loved ones on a regular basis. Block it out in your diary, because as you know, if it does not get scheduled it will not happen.

Tip 2: Technological advantage. While digital connection is not a substitute for in-person interaction, it can still be a great way to stay connected with friends and family who live far away. Remember though that FaceTime and face-to-face time are not the same thing and some things are better analogue.

Tip 3: Pay attention. Better to give someone 15 minutes of your undivided attention, than 30 minutes of half attention. There is nothing worse than talking to someone who is reading emails or typing at the same time. Multitaskers, we see you. When you are talking to someone, give them your full attention. Listen actively and show genuine interest in what they have to say.

Tip 4: Speak up. If you are struggling, feeling isolated or lonely, reach out to someone you trust and let them know what is going on. Chances are they will be happy to support you in any way they can. People are nicer than we give them credit for! Also, if you notice someone is struggling, reach out.

By prioritizing human connection in our lives, we can cultivate a sense of belonging and purpose that will sustain us through even the toughest of times; sometimes we just need someone in the trenches with us. So, pick up the phone, send that message, or give someone a call. You never know how much it might mean to them, and to you.

Ring Ring.

NON-NEGOTIABLE WELLBEING

It's been a long week. We finally arrive at the weekend and we try to squeeze as much in as we can: dinners, dates, daffodil picking (I couldn't think of another D). We have to squeeze every ounce of fun out of it, right? We work hard, we play hard. It's no wonder that you have the Sunday Scaries (the fear of the work week ahead that arrives on Sunday evening) – you haven't stopped for longer than 15 minutes since 2013 when Avicii's *Wake Me Up* was number one in the charts. We are stuck in a never-ending cycle of work and social events, leaving very little or no time for self-care. We tend to overlook our wellbeing, assuming we can always catch up on it later. This approach is not sustainable. Neglecting our physical, emotional and mental health even for a short period of time will undoubtedly have detrimental effects on our productivity, creativity and overall quality of life. No surprises there.

You are definitely not alone in cramming enjoyment into every nook and cranny of your weeks/weekends whenever you have a modicum of free time. I am very much as guilty as you are. To counteract this tendency, I have developed a set of non-negotiables that I adhere to every day, even on the weekend. Yes, even on the weekend. These are activities that I prioritize and do not compromise on, no matter what else is going on in my life. Because I know that as soon as I begin to neglect these activities, I start to suffer physically, mentally and emotionally. Imagine a best self bank account; you can withdraw for a period of time, but eventually you will run out of money and be in debt. You don't want that. You need to ensure you deposit a little bit each day and you will have a healthy balance – check out the activity at the end of the chapter for more.

Of course, life has a habit of throwing curveballs at us, so my non-negotiables are flexible. I adopt a flexibly non-negotiable approach to my wellbeing. While I try my best to stick to them every day, I understand that there will be times when I have to deviate from my non-negotiables. However, I ensure that these instances are the exception rather than the rule. Say I can't go for a walk at 12 because I'm speaking to the publisher and the team about this book (the things I do for you); instead, I will block my calendar out at 4 pm and ensure I go then.

Here are my non-negotiables (yours will be very different and we will work them out in a minute):

Wake up by 6 am – during the week (I treat myself to a lie-in on the weekend if I need it)
Cold water (in the cold tub or shower) – every day
Meditate – every day
Greens and supplements – every day
Gratitude and exploratory writing – every day
Stretch – every day
Workout and/or 10K steps – every day
Morning sunlight/SAD lamp – every day
24-hour fast – one per month
Books – four per month

I do the majority of my non-negotiables first thing in the morning. On the occasions that I re-fold the human burrito, hit snooze and sleep past 7 am, I find that I'm chasing my tail all day. On these days that I sleep in and my morning routine is interrupted, I rarely have the energy, willpower or desire to do my non-negotiables once I have finished work. Therefore, the key habit for me is to get up before 6 am. Swing those legs out. When the feet touch terra firma, I know I am all good and I will have a good day! Consider this when we schedule your non-negotiables in a minute.

Incorporating non-negotiables into your daily routine can help you prioritize your wellbeing, regardless of how busy your week is looking, how many meetings you have tomorrow, or how many parties you have next weekend. However, you can't just take my list, as it won't work for you. What works for Layla will not work for Mo and that is fine. It is important to choose activities that work for you. Time to create your own non-negotiables:

Tip 1: Reflection time. Think back over the past month when you felt your best self, when you were happy, full of energy and running on all cylinders. You know when you just felt like a champion walking down the street, like nothing could knock you off your stride. Write down what you were doing that made you feel that way. Get really clear.

Tip 2: Start small. Take one or two of your non-negotiables as outlined above that will be easy to incorporate into your daily routine and break it/them down into the smallest possible increment. James Clear would call this an atomic habit,[33] e.g. walking in green spaces becomes lacing up your trainers and stepping outside. Seems much more doable, right?

Tip 3: Timing. Make a commitment to do your non-negotiable(s) at the same time every single day. 'Maybe I will do this later' is essentially an acceptance that it will not happen. Remember this is a non-negotiable, not a maybe-potential.

Tip 4: Tracking. What gets measured gets incentivized, gets improved. Write it down and keep yourself honest. I use a Google Sheets habit tracker, which has been massively helpful for me and kept me honest.

Tip 5: Be flexible. Life happens and there will be days when you miss the mark and cannot stick to your non-negotiables. Do not beat yourself up about it; instead, aim to get back on track tomorrow. You've got this.

Tip 6: Experiment. Try out different non-negotiables and see what works best for you. It could be anything from reading to taking a yoga class. What works now may not work next year. This is a good thing, as it means you are growing!

Tip 7: Social accountability. Share your non-negotiables with a friend, family member or even on social media if you are feeling particularly brave. There is nothing like a bit of self-inflicted peer pressure to keep you going.

Tip 8: Stay motivated. Remember why you started in-corporating non-negotiables into your routine, think back to your best self and how that person felt.

I first learned about the best self bank account activity (you can do this on your own or with people) from the incredible Mark Mulligan and it has been a super effective and useful exercise ever since.

We usually spend our time thinking about the external things we want, like the house, the car, partner, job, etc. rather than thinking about why these things are important to us or what we want to get from having them.

There are lots of problems in only focusing on the external things you want in your life. Don't get me wrong: we can aim for external things, I certainly do, but there is more to life than smashing one goal after another without ever feeling the way we want.

Despite all your best efforts, talent and perseverance, life can serve us some unexpected surprises that get in the way. The cost of achieving your ambition may be greater than the payback; you may get there, achieve everything in your external world and realize that it is not giving you what you want.

Q1 – We hit a goal we move on; let's move the dial to how we want to feel when we get there. Let's think about our best selves. So, what I'm going to invite you to do now is to think about things slightly differently. Start with the end achievement in mind and let's think about how we want to feel on the journey.

Q2 – Sometimes people use a single word like 'charged' or 'buzzing'. Some people imagine a character and often phrases like 'on a roll' or 'centred' are quite common. Sometimes it's not even a word, but a feeling that cannot be put into words. People may articulate it with a physical gesture or a sound. If more than one best self may come to mind, fantastic, pick one and focus on that.

Q3 – When you think about this best self, allow yourself to reflect back to a time in the past when you have felt this way. Take yourself back to that time as if you are watching yourself. Where were you? What were you doing? Who if anyone was there with you? Take time to notice: What did you see? What did you hear? What did you smell? How did you feel?

We are now going to discuss the things that have the biggest impact on you and some simple, practical changes that can make an extraordinary difference, using your best self bank account. Some things help you and increase your balance; some things sabotage you and decrease your balance.

Q4 – On a piece of paper, draw one line down the middle. On the left you are going to write 'deposits' and on the right 'withdrawals'. Now, note down what builds up that best self bank account and what puts you into your overdraft.

To help you get the most from this exercise here are some categories to prompt you: exercise, socializing, alcohol, weather, colleagues, friends, purpose, learning, faith, TV, news, phone, social media, sex, food.

Some of the things you call out can be both deposits and withdrawals – do not worry, this is quite normal.

Having completed the exercise, take a few moments to reflect:

Compare the length of the two sides of your account. Which list is longer? What does this mean to you?

If something appears on both sides, what is the difference? What insight does this give you?

Which are the things that are simplest to do or change?

What was the biggest surprise?

What proportion of the things on the lists are within your control? You can circle them.

Q5 – I would like you to make a commitment today to wind up one of your deposits and wind down one of your withdrawals.

Let us build up our best self bank accounts together. If you feel comfortable it can help to share your commitment with friends, family or colleagues, or just keep it to yourself.

One of George Washington's favourite quotes, which I love, is 'Many mickles make a muckle'. I believe Washington was referring to the effect of compound interest.

If you invest £10,000 with an annual interest of 5 per cent, you will have £27,000 after 20 years. We're all familiar with the effect compound interest can have on your savings, but maybe not so much with the effect compound interest can have on your best self bank account. If you improve by 1 per cent every day, compounded daily, that adds up to 3,778 per cent per year, meaning that at the end of the year, you are 38 times better than when you started. Sweet.

You are your priority and it is time for a new attitude to reflect that – a flexibly non-negotiable attitude. Let's go!

12
WORK–LIFE BALANCE DOES NOT EXIST

With the evaporation of the commute and evisceration of any delineation between work and home, it's no wonder that the ping of an email or instant message in the evening strikes fear into even the most ardent of us wellbeing practitioners.

Technology has revolutionized the way we work, no doubt about it. With the rise of digital working, it has become easier than ever to stay connected and work or study from anywhere at any time. This is great news. Someone remind me, why am I still living in the UK rather than somewhere with a sunnier climate? Undoubtedly this has made us 'feel' more productive and efficient. The jury is out on whether we are or not; as technology has proliferated, productivity in the UK has almost stalled, rising by just 2.1 per cent from 2019 to 2023.[34] Are we busy being productive, or are we busy being busy? Remember, an email is just someone else's to-do list. Regardless of our opinion on the productivity debate, technology has undoubtedly blurred the lines between work and personal life, leaving many of us struggling to find a healthy balance between the two.

According to Microsoft, since the pandemic, there has been a 28 per cent increase in after-hours work and a 14 per cent increase in weekend work.[35] Even I cannot find a positive angle on this. With the lines between work and personal life becoming increasingly blurred, it is no surprise that many of us find it difficult to switch off from work. Our bedrooms and front rooms are now also our offices and there is an expectation that we are available almost instantaneously.[36] In the UK, we work from home on average 1.7 days per week, but this flexibility does not come freely. When I work from home, the days feel longer. Without the need to catch the train home, it's much easier to feel obligated to overwork and power through all the emails that have been left unread.

However, it's not all bad news. The same study found that we may be working longer, but we also save two hours of commute time. We spend 40 per cent of this time working, 34 per cent on leisure and 11 per cent on caregiving. So yes, our workdays are elongating, but the increased flexibility is freeing up time for other activities and a life outside of work. I challenge you to find someone who has not done their ironing during a 'company-wide update call'. This all means that we need to work harder to define the boundaries between work and life, as they are not clear anymore. If they exist at all.

Public service announcement: it is time to forget the term work–life balance – it is nonsense. We each live one life and work is just one part of it... and shouldn't be a first priority (think back to your non-negotiables, which happen first thing every morning). The term work–life balance indicates that we can find balance between work and life, that work will play nicely and that life will happen in equal measure. Nope, it doesn't work like that. Work is often much more demanding – deadlines, due dates and deliverables – and life, well that just comes second, it's not even up for debate. Imagine trying to say, 'Sorry boss, I can't do that work, I'm relaxing.' If we do decide to keep a similar term, let us use life–work balance, as life definitely comes first.

I think you can agree that we are facing quite a challenge and I cannot see it abating anytime soon. How do we go about drawing our own lines between work and personal life? My favourite way is to establish clear digital boundaries. Keeping it simple for now, when we finish our workday, we must make a conscious effort to shut down our devices, disconnect from work-related communication and engage in activities that are absolutely not work related. I struggle with this big time, as I have a pretty demanding day job, then in the evening I tend to do my social media work, preparing for speeches and book writing. There comes a point, though, when I just say no and put everything away. Sometimes analogue solutions are best when it comes to digital problems. Boundaries first, balance second.

When I finish work, I shut my laptop, change my glasses from my Harry Potters to my Ryan's evening glasses and get outside for some fresh air – around the block if I am at home or a walk to the tube if I am in the office. As my brother, a formal Royal Marine, once told me: 'There's no bad weather, only bad clothing choices.' This is crucial knowledge living in London where it rains 412 days per year.

I know that if I even peek at my emails and/or respond to one work-related message after I have finished for the day, I will find it almost impossible to switch off and enjoy my evening. By establishing this hard boundary at the end of my day, I am able to draw an invisible line under my working day and begin my evening with a sense of relaxation and ease.

Of course, establishing boundaries in the digital working world is not easy at all. I always want to peek back into the digital cookie jar. 'Just one look won't hurt.' It requires discipline, self-awareness and a willingness to put our own needs first. But by doing so we can reduce our stress levels, improve our wellbeing and ultimately become more productive and effective in both our personal and professional lives. Win–win.

Here are some practical tips to help you establish some boundaries of your own:

Tip 1: I will/will not. Set clear expectations with your colleagues and clients. Let them explicitly know what your working hours are and when you are available, e.g. 'I can't do XX time, as that is when I pick my children up.' This will help to manage their expectations and reduce the likelihood of those dreaded out-of-hours messages.

Tip 2: It's not just work. Do the same with family and friends. After seven hours of staring at my own face on calls, the last thing I want to do is another FaceTime call. 'Sorry, Grandad, but no.' Decline. I will put my headphones in, call you back and head for a walk around the park instead.

Tip 3: Digital balance. Technology is the issue, but also the solution. You probably message more with your boss than you do your boyfriend. As of 2023, some of the best things you can do are (although this will change as the tech evolves): auto-schedule meetings to finish early, silence notifications, focus time, set working hours to limit/ prohibit notifications, set outlook rules to automate/ reduce inbox noise, schedule quiet hours, delay email send, block your lunch break out of office or even let colleagues know they don't need to reply outside their working hours by adopting the following signature – 'I am sending this email at a time that suits me; please do not feel obliged to respond right now, rather at a time that suits you.'

Tip 4: Closing-down routine. Whether it is going for a walk, changing your glasses, taking a bath or practising meditation, find an activity that you can do every day to finish the workday, begin the evening and switch off. Make this a part of your daily evening routine to help establish a clear boundary between work and personal life. Cal Newport, the author of *Digital Minimalism*,[37] actually says 'schedule shutdown complete' when he finishes his routine, which I quite like.

Tip 5: Create physical boundaries. If/when you work from home, create a designated workspace that is separate from your personal space. When you finish the day, pack everything up and move away. Yes, this does mean that you can't work from your bed. OK, you can, just not all the time. Maybe space is at a premium and you do not have a separate space – in that case, pack everything away, make it tidy and move from that part of the room. This is much easier when we are in a physical office and not something we need to consider as much.

By establishing clear boundaries and not leaving it to chance, we can create a healthier and more balanced approach to work and personal life. I did it again – I mean personal life and work. So, tomorrow when you finish work, shut down your laptop, put it away, change your glasses and step outside for some fresh air. Your evening will thank you for it!

13

WANT SOME GREEN?

How much time do you spend outside? It probably isn't as much time as you think. The average person in the United States, for example, spend under two hours outside per day.[38] That is only half a day per week outdoors. And that time is probably spent travelling from one indoor venue to another, breathing exhaust fumes at the traffic lights – ahhh, nature. What we seem to have completely forgotten is that getting into nature is a vital aspect of our overall wellbeing and not just something we do once or twice a month. We were not built to spend our days hidden from the sun, hibernating indoors at the same temperature all year around. 'Who touched the thermostat?'

Nature has a calming and rejuvenating effect on us, providing us with a sense of peace and quiet away from the constant buzz of technology and the stresses of daily life. Even just a short walk in a local park or a quick hike in the woods can help us feel better. When was the last time you took a walk without headphones or your phone? I can't remember either.

According to a study of 20,000 people by the University of Exeter,[39] spending two hours a week in green spaces such as local parks or other natural environments, either all at once or spaced over several visits, can lead to better physical health and psychological wellbeing. The study showed that people who met this two-hour threshold were substantially more likely to report good health and wellbeing than those who did not. This two-hour threshold is a hard boundary, indicating that there are no benefits for people who do not hit the two-hour mark. You know what you need to do.

If that didn't convince you, a 2023 study from Finland[40] found that dropping into a park or other urban green space three or four times per week can cut people's chances of taking medications for anxiety and depression by a third and even reduces the need for asthma medication. This finding highlights the crucial role that nature can play in our mental health and wellbeing. Sometimes simple and ancient solutions are best. Listen to the rustle of the trees, the gentle whistling of the wind, the babbling stream and the leaves skipping across the ground and the problems that seemed massive hours ago will fade away into nothingness.

As Lord Byron wrote in his poem 'Childe Harold's Pilgrimage':

There is a pleasure in the pathless woods,
There is a rapture on the lonely shore,
There is society, where none intrudes,
By the deep sea, and music in its roar:
I love not man the less, but nature more.

Getting into nature doesn't have to be a grand adventure. You don't have to learn bush craft, or bring a tent or transform yourself into Bear Grylls. It can be as simple as taking a walk in a local park or sitting in a nearby green space.

When was the last time you felt a sense of natural awe? Something that took your breath away? You probably can't remember. The Japanese have a wonderful word which captures this sense: yugen. Yugen is the sense of beauty and mystery that is often associated with nature. The word itself is difficult to translate into English, but it is often described as an awareness of the universe that triggers feelings of awe and wonder. It is a feeling that can be elusive in our fast-paced, modern lives, but it is something that can be cultivated.

It doesn't have to come from nature though; for example, in the Japanese tea ceremony, the focus is on creating a serene and peaceful atmosphere that allows the participants to appreciate the beauty of the tea, the utensils and the surroundings. The careful attention to detail and the deliberate movements of the participants can help to create a sense of yugen: a calming sense of feeling the beauty around you. We would all probably benefit from taking the time to slow down and cultivate some yugen today.

As we have explored, even a small amount of time spent in nature can make a significant difference to our sense of wellbeing and cultivate a sense of yugen. It is also important to note that getting into nature does not have to be a solitary activity. Spending time in nature with friends and family can be a great way to connect with others while also reaping the benefits of being outdoors.

Tip 1: Green time. Block it into your calendar and prioritize it. See Chapter 1, 'Taking a stroll', for more on how, when and where to squeeze more green spaces into your life.

Tip 2: 2 for 1. Meeting a friend or taking a 1–1 call? Why not meet in the park or take the call while walking along the river? When making plans, consider if they can be done al fresco.

Tip 3: Bringing nature to you. If you are unable to get out into nature, you can bring nature to you. One study found that working from home with some well-placed house plants can reduce physiological and psychological stress.[41] This is accomplished through suppression of the sympathetic nervous system activity and diastolic blood pressure (yeah that) and promotion of comfortable, soothed and natural feelings. So, if you can't get outside for a walk, you can still experience some of the benefits by bringing nature to you. But what about if you are not naturally green fingered, forget to water your plants and struggle to keep them alive? You could consider getting a cactus, which provides the same stress-reducing benefits but is less likely to die.

As we have discussed, it is essential to make a conscious effort to spend more time outdoors, even if it is just a few minutes each day. This will soon add up to the two-hour target mark. Whether it's taking a walk in a local park or sitting in a green space, remember there is no bad weather, only bad clothing choices. And even if you are not able to get outside, you can always bring nature to you.

Time for us to embrace our inner naturists. But no... not like that!

Despite appearances, most days I am just about holding it together. I often feel so anxious I could pop. I have had anxiety on and off for years and took medication for it multiple times during my teens and twenties.

I have my dream job, speak on big stages around the world and share my story pretty openly on social media, but every day is still a challenge, as it is for all of us. I feel anxious pretty much every day, that much has not really changed. I think I will always be like that and I'm not upset about it. Not anymore anyway. I have just learned how to deal with my anxiety and funnel it into excitement and energy. 'Oh, hello old friend. Back again, are we?'

Here's a scenario. You are about to go on a job interview; you have an elevated heart rate, butterflies in your stomach, sweaty palms, you are nervous. Are you excited or are you anxious?

There is a fine line between anxiety and excitement (I'm not discussing anxiety disorders here). Physiologically, the two are almost identical; both sets of symptoms result from the arousal of the nervous system. So, anxiety and excitement create essentially the same physical sensations – we just label them differently.

The more scared or anxious we are of doing something, speaking to someone, a piece of work, etc, the more sure we can be that we have to do it. Writing this book, putting myself out there, is anxiety inducing for sure, which is why I knew I needed to move toward it. Same with learning how to dance salsa; I could not think of anything worse, which is why I'm going to go.

Stephen Pressfield, in *The War of Art*,[42] shares with us that:

> Resistance is experienced as fear; the degree of fear equates
> to the strength of Resistance. Therefore the more fear we feel
> about a specific enterprise, the more certain we can be that that
> enterprise is important to us and to the growth of our soul.
> That's why we feel so much Resistance. If it meant nothing to
> us, there'd be no Resistance.

Turn toward it and look it square in the face.

OK, but what does that mean in real life? Let us take the number one fear in the world: public speaking. Did you know that people are more scared of public speaking than death, zombies and clowns? Why have there been no horror films of the big stage, bright lights and a microphone with a lust for blood? Maybe I'll move into writing fiction, right after the book tour. As I mentioned beforehand, I do a lot of public speaking and have spoken to some pretty large audiences of over 1,500 people. I may look like I'm having fun and that I'm a natural, but what is happening on the outside is certainly not reflected internally. My anxiety pre-speaking used to manifest itself in making me feel like I was going to wet myself. I have not felt that in years but it hit me hard on stage recently – I almost walked off.

How should you deal with anxiety when public speaking?

Tip 1: Your personal canary. The feelings we mentioned earlier are often trying to tell you that something is going on. Stop for a second and explore what this insight could be. You could consider these feelings your own personal canary in the coal mine. In the 20th century, coal miners brought canaries into the mines as an early warning signal for toxic gases, primarily carbon monoxide. The birds, being more sensitive, would become sick before the miners, who would then have a chance to escape or put on protective respirators. Hmm, my heart rate is elevated and my breath feels heavy – the canary is chirping away. Stop and ask yourself why that may be. As Steven Pressfield says, this could just be the resistance rearing its head – which means we move towards it – or it could be because the mine is about to collapse and we need to get out of there. Either way, we stop, listen and assess the situation. With the public speaking example, it is the resistance talking and I just need to get started, move around, laugh and pick a friendly face out of the crowd. 'Thanks, Tweetie Pie, false alarm.'

Tip 2: You are doing great. Remind yourself, you are not as much of a piece of rubbish as you think you are. You wouldn't be there otherwise. Your nerves just mean that you care and that's why you will smash it.

Tip 3: Point at the elephant. I like to address my anxiety or nerves directly when I'm on stage – 'Hey, look over there everyone, it's a massive elephant!' It makes me feel less like I'm going to wet myself in front of everyone – 'Blimey, there are a lot of people here, anyone else pee a little? Just me? No worries!'

Tip 4: Turn anxiety into excitement. As we mentioned, anxiety and excitement manifest in similar ways and I make a conscious choice to embrace these feelings and increased levels of energy instead of trying to suppress them, which never works. When I present/speak sitting down, I feel like I'm going to explode with nerves. If I get up and move around it helps the energy dissipate and I feel it is much more engaging as well.

Tip 5: Box breathing. I do this to control the nerves before going out. In for 4–6 seconds, hold, out, hold, repeat. See Chapter 5, 'And breathe', for more on this.

Tip 6: Just get started. Often it is the first step we are most worried about – take the leap of faith, you got this. I go from needing the toilet backstage to exhilaration in minutes after I step out. Smile, have some fun and run through the tips above. You and others have survived this and you will again!

Do the thing you are resisting the most. Do it bolder and louder than you are comfortable with. Give yourself completely, with energy and enthusiasm. Do it long enough that you are no longer held back by it, and your relationship to it is transformed.

Ask the person out, do the speech, go dancing. Whatever it is you have been putting off, now it is time to dive in.

INSTANTLY UNAVAILABLE

On average, we receive 63.5 notifications per day[43] and check our phones 352 times per day.[44] We are constantly on and always available. However, just because a message is instant it does not mean your response has to be. We can be contacted via a multitude of platforms, methods and means of communication, with every message, comment and call being beamed directly into the palm of our hand. That may soon change, as they will be beamed directly into your brain via neural link. 'Ahhh, much better, I don't have to use my thumbs now.' Even Aldous Huxley and George Orwell wouldn't have seen this coming.

New York Times bestselling author Neal Stephenson has sold over 3 million books and is no doubt a prolific fiction writer – his most well-known book is probably *Snowcrash*. Given his success, he unsurprisingly gets a lot of emails, invites and letters and doesn't respond to >99 per cent of them. He is not being intentionally rude or particularly enjoying giving readers the cold shoulder (sorry, couldn't help myself), but high-quality work requires high-quality uninterrupted focus. It is this author's belief that the same can be considered for our personal wellbeing – a state of high-quality, individual wellbeing requires us to disconnect. In more ways than one.

Neal asks, 'Would you rather a bunch of well-meaning emails or a novel?'[45] A novel which could be around for years and be read by millions. He would rather be a good novelist, and hopes that you can forgive him for being a bad correspondent. Replace the word novel with a different focus. He says we can do one or the other, not both. Yes, we are not as famous as Neal, but if we are constantly TikToking, Tweeting, Instagramming, WhatsApping and Snapchatting for hours and hours per week, how are we expecting to do the things we need to do to be our best self? We can't.

It's my mission to engage 1 billion people in the betterment of wellbeing. Consequently, I have to turn up regularly on social media to engage and grow my audience in order to reach as many people as possible. I sometimes get up to 30 DMs per day. I really do try my best to respond to all, especially people who have put in a bit of effort. If only my dating profile was as successful. I want to help as many people as I can and I always respect the hustle, but if I took every 'Can I grab 30 mins of your time?' request, I would be working 47 hours per day. I simply can't do it. OK, maybe not 47 hours, but yesterday I added up that I was asked for a total of four hours, 20 mins of time. In addition to working nine hours yesterday, this would have made for a very long day and would have left little to no time for what I need.

You could consider the following activities to become a little more instantly unavailable:

Tip 1: Make an effort. You don't need to respond to copy and pastes, sales messages and/or every email you receive. When someone does their homework, I will try my best to make time. However, this will be at a time that suits me, often when walking after lunch. Remember that an email is essentially someone else's to-do list and people are often taking the path of least resistance, which is to ask you to do something instead of doing it themselves. 'If you want something doing, ask the busy person.'

Tip 2: Not now. You don't need to respond immediately; just because a message is instant, doesn't mean that you need to be. Leave a message on double blue ticks, it really doesn't matter. Seriously, try it.

Tip 3: Leverage. Instead of having multiple 1–1 calls, chats and conversations, I have focused on increasing my leverage, where I can speak to multiple people at once. 'Of course I can explain what I do, I host XX event every month – details here.' This saves an incredible amount of time and creates a community at the same time.

Tip 4: Timeboxing effort. Some of my more militant digitally minimalist friends have windows of time when they are available for chats, calls, messages, social media, etc. I have received out of office messages from them, saying, 'Thanks for your message, I use my phone during XX hours, I will respond then.' Respect.

Tip 5: The IOOOO/In Office Out of Office. Put your OOO on when you are in the office to create space for in-person interactions. 'I am in the office today, so you might see a slight delay in my IM and email replies, as I am making the most of seeing people face to face. I will be in the XX area if you want to come and say hello at XX time. I will be back in the home office on XX, and will have more of an online presence again then.' This was a world first when I created it a year or so ago and was well adopted.

Time to become a little more unavailable, focus on the things in your life that make you happy and healthy – unless that is responding to messages instantaneously, in which case please carry on. I am sure your friends, family and loved ones will forgive you for being a bad correspondent.

No one cares as much as you. No one. You have to send a difficult email, you worry all weekend about how it will be received. You make a faux pas in a presentation and struggle to sleep, as it's on repeat in your head. You have a discussion with a colleague that ends without resolution and you are still thinking about it until late Sunday night. Try as you might, you worry your actions will cause this or that drama/ negative outcome. 'Why would I do that, I'm so stupid!'

Imagine a scenario where you have just sat through an incredible performance of *Hamilton* in London's West End and at the end of the musical the spotlight shines only on the lead actor, exposing every move they make to the audience and ignoring every other actor. Most of us go through life believing that we are that lead actor, constantly in the spotlight with the public watching our every move; this causes a lot of anxiety and an overwhelming sense of pressure to always be perfect.

However, in the real world outside of your solipsistic reality (the view or theory that the self is all that can be known to exist), everyone is playing out their own version of this drama in their own head and you are definitely not the protagonist. No one cares as much as you do. They are worried about the mistake they just made, the error they think everyone is thinking and gossiping about: 'I just commuted all the way to work and said hello to my boss with my zipper down, I must be the most stupid man alive.' At least I had my favourite boxers on.

This common phenomenon is called the spotlight effect. It is the cognitive bias that makes you believe that the whole world is watching you. We often believe that other people are watching with a keener eye than they actually are! A psychological study highlighted the spotlight effect when it comes to our appearance.[46] In this study, they asked people to wear one shirt that was flattering and one that was not so flattering. According to the study, participants expected that 50 per cent of people would take notice of the unattractive shirt, but in reality, only 25 per cent did. Similarly, when it came to the attractive outfit, the expected attention was overestimated. This indicates that we tend to overestimate how much attention others pay to us.

The researchers wanted to test whether this applied to more than just appearance. This probably will not surprise you, but they found that this overestimation also held true for athletic and video game performance.[47] People did not notice the successes or failures of the participants as much as they thought they would. In other words, the data suggests that we tend to live in our own self-perception bubbles. Surprised?

So, let us explore how to turn off the spotlight and exit stage right to rapturous applause:

Tip 1: Self-acceptance. It's time to embrace your weirdness, quirks and unique traits; they make you who you are and that is not going to change. You are not as terrible as you think and some people may even like your loud laugh. Some people. Not me.

Tip 2: So what? When you find yourself ruminating on the fact that someone may have just noticed the toilet paper that had attached itself to your foot as you came out of the toilet, ask yourself, 'So what?' What happens if someone does notice and who cares anyway? It's funny. It's not the end of the world. You will feel the nerves dissipate by the second and you will probably laugh that it is the third time you have done it this week.

Tip 3: From imagination to reality. Instead of imagining that others are judging you, why not take a second and look/listen to see if anyone actually cares? Chances are, they don't; they are currently under their own spotlight. If you want to go really crazy, ask them, 'Did you just notice that I slipped up on the second sentence of the third paragraph on the fourth slide?' By the time you finish the question, you won't need to wait for the response.

Tip 4: You are not the star. You are the star in one show and one show only. Yes, that is your own. Take solace in the fact that there are 8 billion other shows going on, with their own dramas, stories and mishaps, and you do not have to perform all the time. No one is watching anyway.

Send the email, make the mistake, have the discussion. Try not to worry; no one else is – not as much as you, anyway.

FEELING SAD? TIME FOR HYGGE

You wake up, it's dark. You go to work, it's dark. You finish work, it's dark. If you are lucky, you will see 47 seconds of sunshine as it flickers through the blinds as you reminisce about the last time you felt the sun's warm kiss on your skin. Sigh. In sunny old England, from October onward, the days grow shorter quickly and by the winter solstice in late December, it can feel like we don't see the sun for weeks on end. I won't complain too much though, as in Iceland in the peak of winter they only get 3.5 hours of sun per day.

As the sleep psychologist Guy Meadows states, 'The arrival of winter brings with it a number of potential challenges for sleep, including reduced exposure to sunlight, cooler temperatures, clock changes, and lowered immunity… All these factors disturb sleep, making it harder to get up in the morning.'[48] These changes result in subsequent hormonal changes; unhealthy behaviours and certain vitamin deficiencies can also be behind the onset of seasonal fatigue.

For some people, this goes beyond just a slight drop in mood or energy and can make life very unpleasant for months on end. This is seasonal affective disorder/SAD, which a third of us in the UK suffer with, affecting more women than men: 'It is like having your own portable black cloud.'[49] This is due to the fact that we produce less serotonin in the winter, the hormone often tied to mood. Additionally, we produce more melatonin, the hormone that regulates sleep and maintains the body's circadian rhythm. This is because the brain's pineal gland, which is usually triggered by darkness to produce melatonin, produces more in the winter as a result of the shorter days and reduced sunlight.

This should mean that countries closer to the poles with less sunlight are less happy, right? Wrong. According to the World Happiness Report 2022,[50] the top three happiest nations on earth are Finland, Denmark and Iceland – hardly equatorial or known for their white sandy beaches. The Danes attribute their collective happiness to the practice of hygge, meaning 'to give courage, comfort, joy'.[51] Hygge is thought to have stemmed from the old Norse words *hygga* – to comfort, *hugge* – to embrace and *hugr* – mood. It does not have a direct translation to English, but the most common translation is cosiness. I like to think of it as a cosiness of the soul, kind of like a hug, just without the physical touch. Something like this:

Burning logs crackle.

The aroma of coffee drifts through the room.

You're warm and cosy, surrounded by your friends and family.

You're living in the moment.

Not worried about the future and not about fretting the past.

That's hygge.[52]

If you're looking to fight off those winter blues and keep SAD at bay, let us inject some warmth and comfort into your life with the following top tips for a hygge-filled winter:

Tip 1: Cosiness. Create the perfect cosy environment: candles, candles, candles. Fill your home with soft lighting and make it warm and inviting. Choose soft furnishings and accessories that add warmth and texture to your living space.

Tip 2: Hibernation. Bury yourself under a nice thick blanket or invest in a cosy throw that you can wrap yourself up in and snuggle down with a good book or movie. It is cold and dark, no one is going to see you – wear your comfiest clothes: hoodies, sweatpants, slippers and even that hat your nan knitted for you. 'Thanks Nan, I love it…'

Tip 3: Hot and soupy. Indulge in wintery culinary treats; it's time for hot chocolate, soups, pumpkin spiced lattes and porridges. Say goodbye to salads and embrace the warmth of hearty, comforting food. No guilt – I'll worry about my love handles when I feel the sun again.

Tip 4: Take time to relax. Combine all of the above with a Netflix binge, or other wintery activities. Lean into it and don't fight it. Whether it's curling up with a good book, watching a movie or going for a winter walk, embrace the season and enjoy it to the fullest.

Tip 5: Light therapy. Invest in a sunrise alarm clock or therapy lamp to help boost your mood and energy levels. I use the sunrise alarm clock and therapy lamp every single morning for 20 minutes, even in the summer. It's also often suggested that everyone should consider taking a vitamin D supplement during the winter months when we're deprived of sunlight.

Tip 6: Winter sun. Schedule and protect time to walk for at least 30 minutes when the sun is up (optimistic for London in winter, but get out regardless). Block out your calendar, wrap up warm, and get yourself to the park or countryside to soak up some natural light. Remember, as my brother Scott said to me, 'There's no bad weather, only bad clothing choices.'

By using these pumpkin spicy tips, you can roll into the warm embrace of hygge and keep the winter blues at bay. So light some candles, wrap yourself up in a cosy blanket and indulge in some winter treats – it is time to get your hygge on!

18

FURUSATO

For years, there was nothing I wanted to do more than escape my hometown. My hometown being Hastings, which is a seaside town in the southeast of the UK and by all measures is quite lovely. Ten years ago I moved away, moving in the opposite direction to the hordes of people who left the city for a quieter life on the coast; my family/friends tell me that Hastings is being gentrified rather quickly by the DFLs – the 'Down From Londons', so I must be a UTL – Up To London. For years and years I was unable to disassociate certain parts of my past from the place of my birth and struggled to go back even for a couple of days. I no longer feel this way – rather, I feel a very strong affinity to my hometown and love to spend the weekend by the sea, enjoying the fresh air, the sound of the seagulls and walks on the stones. I have developed a deep sense of Furusato, which is a concept that we will explore together and build into our days.

The feelings I used to hold toward my place of birth were not only painful, but run counter to a pretty famous curse that was placed on the town about 100 years ago by Aleister Crowley – a famous magician who was labelled 'the wickedest man in the world' and a Satanist by the popular press at the time. Crowley apparently used to sacrifice animals, made furniture out of human skin and is said to still haunt the town. Seems like a nice guy. Crowley's curse says that if you have lived in Hastings you can never leave, and if you try you will always come back. The only way to truly leave is to take with you a stone with a hole in it from the beach – also known as a hag stone. Either that or years of mental illness, injuries and troublesome memories. They'll keep you away.

Hastings is not just famous for Satanists and wellbeing aficionados, but was the birthplace of television, the scene of the Battle of Hastings in 1066 (which actually happened in Battle, but the Battle of Battle sounds strange) and has been the residence of Alan Turing, the Duke of Wellington, Lewis Carroll, Beatrix Potter and Elizabeth Blackwell.

So, Furusato. Furusato is a Japanese word that can be translated as 'hometown' or 'birthplace'. But for the Japanese people it has a much deeper meaning than just a physical location. Furusato is a concept that represents the emotional and cultural ties that a person has to their place of origin and the feelings of nostalgia and longing that come with being away from it. Kind of like homesickness, but a more positive version of it.

In Japan, the idea of Furusato is deeply ingrained in the culture. People often have a strong attachment to their hometowns, even if they have moved away for work or other reasons. This attachment is expressed in many ways, such as the traditional festivals and customs that are unique to each region and the special foods and products that are associated with specific areas. I'm not sure how attached I feel to the food from Hastings. Now, don't get me wrong, the fish and chips are good, but the food in London is better. For me it is the old Georgian pubs; my favourite is Ye Olde Pumphouse – check it out if you ever go to Hastings. It's the smell of the sea, the fresh air, the jokes that 'you had to be there for' with old friends, the nod you give people that you have known since you were six but still can't remember the name of. All of this is what made me, me.

Furusato is not just a concept for the Japanese people. It's a universal feeling that can be experienced by anyone who has ever left their hometown and felt a sense of longing for the place where they grew up. It's a reminder that no matter where we go in life, our roots and our history will always be a part of us. So, whether you are living in your Furusato or away from it, take some time to appreciate the cultural and emotional ties that you have to your birthplace. Celebrate the unique customs and traditions that make your hometown special and take pride in the fact that you are a part of its history and its future.

How can you cultivate some Furusato today?

Tip 1: Find your own hag stone. I assume you don't come from a place that has a curse on it and need to keep your own hag stone. My grandad has collected three for me from his dog walks – surely that is enough to satisfy Aleister's curse. I have the stones on a shelf near where I work and they don't keep me away, rather they remind me of my Furusato and make me smile. Think about what reminds you of where you are from. What is your hometown known for? Get some of it and put it on display.

Tip 2: A home from home. When I go home now, I stay in a bed and breakfast; I treat it like a little holiday and take people with me who haven't been there before. This way, I have to go into tour guide mode and I can see my hometown with a fresh set of eyes, giving me an appreciation for what I took for granted for years.

Tip 3: 'You remember that time?' There is nothing like old friends. Nothing. Life is busy, there are kids, jobs, relationships and none of us have any time. Make time. My friends and I have a couple of dates a year that are set in stone – the St Patrick's Day Mystery Tour (we give one person the money and he books a trip somewhere) and Christmas drinks. It is the most I laugh all year; no one knows you like they do, do not forget that. 'Do you remember the time that…?'

It took a Japanese concept and multiple hag stones to rekindle my love for the southeast. No matter where you are in the world, you can always cultivate a little Furusato. Your Furusato is why you are who you are and you are awesome.

19
KINTSUGI

Vulnerability is courage in you, but weakness in me. Imagine this: someone close to you shares something painful that has happened to them, their story, some trauma that they have been through and you think, 'Wow, that's amazing, how brave, what can I do to help?' Now flip that around and consider being equally vulnerable – I bet your stomach has just done a somersault and you would rather walk over flaming hot coals than do the same.

It's time to shift our perspective on imperfections. They are not something to be ashamed of, but rather gifts to be embraced and worked with. Every experience you have had, every supposed/imagined flaw you possess, every trip, stumble and fall makes you who you are. And let us be real, who wants to be like everyone else anyway? You may occasionally chip and break and need repairs. And that is fine. Find me an inspirational person who has not been 12 rounds. I will wait.

The Japanese have a beautiful way of embracing flaws and imperfections: the art of Kintsugi. It's a technique where broken pottery pieces are repaired with gold, creating an even stronger, more beautiful piece of art, highlighting the cracks as part of the aesthetically pleasing design. Every break is unique and instead of repairing an item like new, the 400-year-old technique actually highlights the scars as a part of the design. Using this as a metaphor for healing ourselves teaches us an important lesson: in the process of repairing things that have broken, we actually create something even more unique, beautiful and resilient.

A Japanese legend tells the story of a mighty shogun warrior who broke his favourite tea bowl and sent it away for repairs. When he received it back, the bowl was held together by unsightly metal staples. Although he could still use it, the shogun was disappointed. Still hoping to restore his beloved bowl to its former beauty, he asked a craftsman to find a more elegant solution. The craftsman wanted to try a new technique, something that would add to the beauty of the bowl as well as repair it. So, he mended every crack in the bowl with a lacquer resin mixed with gold. When the tea bowl was returned to the shogun, there were streaks of gold running through it, telling its story and, the warrior thought, adding to its value and beauty. This method of repair became known as Kintsugi.

Kintsugi, which roughly translates to 'golden joinery', is the Japanese philosophy that the value of an object is not in its beauty, but in its imperfections, and that these imperfections are something to celebrate, not hide.

Trust me, I know first-hand that it is not easy to open up about our own struggles and we can feel weak, vulnerable and embarrassed just at the thought of opening up. It took me years to tell anyone apart from my mum about my battle with bulimia. I also know that mental health issues are more common than we think, especially given how many conversations I have with people who appear to 'have it all together'. I am going to tell you a secret: we are all making it up as we go along. It has taken years and years, but I have learned that my mental trials and tribulations do not make me weak, they make me incredibly unique. In fact, I'm one in a million. This is not just hyperbole either, I actually am. Bear with me. What you have been through is nothing to be ashamed of; it has made you into the resilient human that you are. You are still here and you are still fighting. If you can go through all of that, then there is no limit to what you can achieve. There is no tougher battle than the one you will fight in your own head. None.

Did you know that the likelihood of a man having bulimia is 0.5 per cent,[53] depression is 12.5 per cent,[54] anxiety is 20 per cent[55] and agoraphobia is 0.8 per cent?[56] And if you multiply all those together, the likelihood of having all of these issues is one in a million. You guessed it, I have experienced all of these. I've always been special, I just didn't realize how special. Lucky eh? I feel fortunate to have been through these things and come through the other side, as a lot of people do not. At the time, I would have done anything to be someone else, but I would not change a thing now. I have broken and cracked so many times that I am more gold glue than plate at this point; I am very strong and extremely sparkly and so are you. So, if you are going through something, know you are most definitely not alone and you are a freaking warrior. A golden one at that.

Time to get the gold paint out – here are some practical tips:

Tip 1: Acknowledge your imperfections. The first step to embracing your imperfections is to acknowledge them. You are not perfect, but neither is anyone, apart from me (kidding). Your imperfections are what make you special. As we said, who wants to be like everyone else anyway?

Tip 2: Work out your Kintsugi number. Multiply the likelihood that you will go through X, Y or Z together, ascertain exactly how special you are and wear it with pride. A quick Google search will yield the information you need. 'What is the prevalence of bulimia in men in the UK?' then repeat and multiply the likelihoods together: $0.005 \times 0.125 \times 0.2 \times 0.08 = 0.00001$ or one in a million.

Tip 3: Turn weakness into strength. Instead of seeing your imperfections as weaknesses, see them as a source of strength. The challenges you have faced in your life have made you stronger and more resilient. Take a second to consider all you have been through and think to yourself, 'Wow, if I've been through all of that and I'm still going, yeah, I guess I am pretty tough!' Yes, you are.

Tip 4: Practise self-compassion. Treat yourself with the same kindness and compassion you would offer to a friend. When you make a mistake or experience a setback, be gentle with yourself. Remember that it's ok to be imperfect.

Remember, in the process of repairing things that have 'broken', we actually create something more unique, beautiful and resilient.

Sparkle, my friend.

Do you have your workday planned out for tomorrow? Do you know what time you need to be in the office and what time your first meeting or appointment is? Of course you do. But have you planned your meals, exercise and downtime for tomorrow? Most people overlook this part of our routine, but it is crucial for living a happy, healthy, productive life and often it is the first thing to be dropped when we get busy. In this chapter, we will explore how small daily habits and routines can have a big impact on your wellbeing.

You might have laughed to yourself when I asked if you had planned your meals, sleep, etc tomorrow and thought, 'Good one, Ryan. I'm probably going to demolish a sandwich in 7.3 seconds, walk to the fridge and back 14 times before going to bed at midnight.' Who would want to live out of Tupperware, go to the gym every day or have a set bedtime? You are far too carefree for that and you do not have time either. You're not an athlete or a Benedictine monk, so why would you need to live such a strict and boring life, right?

A disciplined life is a free life. Hear me out. We spend a little time and effort today on our wellbeing, so that we can live a healthy, happy life tomorrow. We can try anyway. We cannot account for the unpredictable, but we can stack the odds in our favour:

We follow a healthy diet today to reduce the chance of sickness later.

We stretch today to prevent injury later.

We meditate today to increase our calm later.

We save a couple of £ today to ease financial worries later.

You get it.

You pay a little now or you pay big later. Your choice. 'Small habits do not add up, they compound. You don't need to be twice as good to get twice the results. You just need to be slightly better.'[57]

This is hardly revolutionary stuff, but eating, sleeping, resting, moving and hydrating well will make you a more productive, happy and healthy individual. I could quote endless studies, but you know this already. Getting off of your ass is better than sitting on it all day, eating an apple is better than a chocolate bar and speaking to a loved one is better than being isolated. You know this already. By being health-ish today (selfish about your health), you can prevent health problems and the time and money that they inevitably cost you down the road. You simply cannot afford not to have a routine. We must treat our wellbeing with the order and discipline it deserves today, or we will be forced to tomorrow... or some time in the distant future, but it is coming. All debts will be paid. In full.

It might seem like a lot of effort, but the formula is pretty simple: small, wellbeing-based habits and activities done daily and consistently throughout the year will undoubtedly result in personal happiness, health, productivity and longevity. Plan your day like an accountant, apply the formula and watch that personal bank account of yours grow – see Chapter 11, 'Non-negotiable wellbeing', for the best self bank account activity.

No matter your goals or aspirations, whether it's Couch to 5K, losing seven pounds, learning German or simply feeling happy and healthy, the answer is in developing a routine. Brad Stulberg says:

> You don't have to feel great, or even good for that matter, to act. Sure, a consistent practice may take at least a little motivation to get going, but over time the equation is reversed. Dedicating yourself to the practice, no matter how you feel, is what builds motivation. The practice is what makes you feel good and changes your mindset, not the other way around.[58]

So, how do we build a routine that works for us? One effective approach is habit stacking, which was coined by BJ Fogg:

Tip 1: Habit stacking. Take your desired behaviour and break it into its smallest possible increments; think about what time of day you want to do it, write down what you currently do at that time of day: e.g. I get up, I brush my teeth, I make my coffee, etc in order – insert your new desired micro habit in between existing habits: after/before (current habit) I will (new habit). For example:

- After I pour my cup of coffee each morning, I will meditate for one minute.
- After I take off my work shoes, I will immediately change into my workout clothes.
- After I sit down to dinner, I will say one thing I'm grateful for that happened today.
- After I get into bed at night, I will give my partner a kiss.

Tip 2: One at a time. Do not set yourself up for failure by setting multiple unattainable goals. Start with something manageable and build from there; get that momentum moving. No one has ever got up off the couch, nailed a marathon, while at the same time quitting smoking and cutting back on the wine. That is a lie – some have, but many more have failed.

Tip 3: Make it enjoyable. If you hate running, don't force yourself into a pair of running shoes and start pounding the streets; you don't want shin splints, trust me. Don't do it to yourself. Find an activity you enjoy, and build that into your routine.

Tip 4: Minimum viable effort. Mike Tyson famously said, 'Discipline is doing what you hate, but doing it like you love it'. So let's follow Iron Mike's lead and stick to our routines when we're in the mood, and especially when we're not. Do something every day, build the momentum and scale the intensity later. If you can't find the energy to fully commit to a difficult task, find a way to maintain the momentum. Can't bring yourself to attend your Spanish class? No worries, watch an episode of Narcos instead. Listen to yourself though – sometimes rest is required. There is a difference between truly needing a rest and a can't-be-bothered attitude, and it's important to learn the difference.

Tip 5: Front loading. I prioritize the things that make me my best self each morning; that is Ryan time. If I leave it until the evening to decide whether I am going to go to the gym or not, more often than not I'm too tired and it won't happen.

Tip 6: Same time. Ignore the above if you are not a morning person. The most important thing is that you pick a time and stick to it. If you leave it up to chance every day, it won't happen. Be honest with yourself.

We either pay a little now, or we pay big later – which is it to be?

21

COSMIC INSIGNIFICANCE THERAPY

You are totally and completely unimportant and that is a wonderful thing. The common consensus is that to live a life worth living, our lives need to involve deeply impressive accomplishments or that they should have a lasting impact on future generations. What a burden we put on our shoulders. No wonder you have a backache. Time for some therapy – some cosmic insignificance therapy. Let us zoom out and remember how little we matter, on a cosmic timescale – how completely irrelevant we are in the grand scheme of things.

The anxieties that clutter the average life, our lives – looming deadlines at work, relationship troubles, money worries – shrink instantly down to irrelevance against the vastness of the cosmos. Even pandemics and politics pale in comparison to the cosmos, which carries on regardless. And breathe. We are here but for the blink of an eye – a mere 4,000 weeks, according to Oliver Burkeman in his excellent book *Four Thousand Weeks: Time management for mortals*, which we are going to unpack a bit further together. Time to take that pressure off and enjoy.

The truth is, our time on this planet is incomprehensibly short compared to the vast expanse of cosmic history. While the universe is 13.7 billion years old, we are a bit more recent. Homo sapiens have been around for just 200,000 years. Think about it this way: if we compressed the entire duration of the universe into the span of a day, with the Big Bang occurring at midnight, humans would arrive late, very late – at 11.59.56 pm to be precise, just four seconds before the clock strikes midnight.[59]

What we know as human civilization, however, has only been going for 6,000 years. According to philosopher Bryan Magee, the golden age of the Egyptian pharaohs happened only 35 lifetimes ago, Jesus was born 20 lifetimes ago, and Henry VIII sat on the English throne a mere five lifetimes ago.[60] That's a blink of an eye in the grand scheme of things. Welcome to your insignificance.

While this realization might be somewhat disorienting or even terrifying, it can also be oddly comforting. Burkeman calls this cosmic insignificance therapy, a term that I love. When life gets overwhelming, to take a step back and realize how small we are in the grand scheme of things can actually be very liberating. All of a sudden our everyday worries and anxieties pale in comparison to the vastness of the cosmos. OK, so maybe the fact that you accidentally sent an email that started out 'Dead colleagues…' is not going to be the end of the world – funny for everyone on CC though. The former bishop of Edinburgh, Richard Holloway, quoted by Burkeman, captures it perfectly: 'The massive indifference of the universe' can be consoling in a strange way.

This does not mean that our lives are completely meaningless. Rather, it's a healthy reminder that the things we worry about on a day-to-day basis, like a disagreement with a client, relationship troubles or money worries, are ultimately insignificant, even if it doesn't feel like it at the time. It's a call to focus on what really matters, to let go of the things that do not and to embrace the fleeting beauty of life – you are not here for very long.

But here is the catch: most of us do not live with this perspective and such carefree abandon. How could you? You have 32,742 unread emails. Instead, we tend to see ourselves as central to the unfolding of the universe. I am still certain that I am in some weird kind of Truman show. It's not just megalomaniacs, solipsists, narcissists, you and me who fall into this trap, it's a fundamental part of being human. After all, from our own perspective, the few thousand weeks we are around do feel like the most important thing in the world.

Psychologists call this the 'egocentricity bias', and it makes sense from an evolutionary standpoint. If we did not have this sense of our own importance, we might be less motivated to fight to survive and propagate our genes. But it also means that we tend to set the bar for a meaningful life way too high. We think we need to accomplish great things, leave a lasting impact on the world or transcend the mundane in order to feel like our lives were well lived. In reality, though, that is not the case. You don't need to be a world-famous celebrity or a Nobel Prize winner to live a meaningful life. Instead, you can focus on the things that bring you joy and fulfilment, whether that is spending time with loved ones, pursuing a career that brings you a sense of eudaimonia (check out Chapter 34, 'Happiness vs joy', for more on eudaimonia), a hobby in ornithology (bird watching) or making a positive impact on your community by volunteering once a week in a local soup kitchen. That is a life well lived.

The truth is, even if your life is relatively small in the grand scheme of things, it can still be full of meaning and purpose. After all, what's the point of leaving a lasting impact if you didn't enjoy the journey and help a few people along the way? You won't be here to enjoy it after you're gone, anyway.

Time for some cosmic insignificance therapy:

Tip 1: Perspective. When you find yourself becoming overwhelmed, ask yourself: 'Will this matter in 1, 2, 5, 10 years? What about 1,000?'

Tip 2: Beauty in the mundane. Don't discount the value of the mundane. Our days can be unremarkable, but it's the little moments of joy and contentment in them that add up to a life well lived. So, keep an eye open for them: catching an elevator as it closes, putting on a T-shirt as it comes out of the tumble dryer, receiving a message from a colleague you have not spoken to in years, etc.

Tip 3: Natural awe. Seeking out experiences that remind you of the vastness of the cosmos can really help to put your problems into perspective. It does for me, anyway. Watching a starry night sky (or an orange-tinged sky in London due to the light pollution), sitting by a lake or river watching the water flow or taking a walk in the woods can be powerful ways to experience awe and remind yourself of your tiny place in the universe. There is an oak tree near me that is over 500 years old and when I walk past it, I like to think to myself how fortunate I am to live here and now. I write this as I sit here with a nice warm coffee, typing away on my Mac as it rains outside, rather than dying in agony with the bubonic plague in 1666.

Mr Burkeman, bring us home please:

Cosmic insignificance therapy is an invitation to face the truth about your irrelevance in the grand scheme of things. To embrace it, to whatever extent you can. (Isn't it hilarious, in hindsight, that you ever imagined things might be otherwise?)

Truly doing justice to the astonishing gift of a few thousand weeks is not a matter of resolving to 'do something remarkable' with them. In fact, it entails precisely the opposite: refusing to hold them to an abstract and over-demanding standard of remarkableness, against which they can only ever be found wanting, and taking them instead on their own terms, dropping back down from godlike fantasies of cosmic significance into the experience of life as it concretely, finitely – and often enough, marvellously – really is.[61]

22

THE AUTHENTIC HERO

Does it ever feel like you're a square peg trying to fit into a round hole?

For most of my life, I have always been a bit different, a bit odd. Find me someone who isn't. I always felt I needed to act, behave, speak differently to fit in. Bumbling through life with a fake smile, but deeply unhappy with who I am, how I look. 'How does everyone else look so composed and I am such a clown?' For years, I forced myself to be completely extroverted, where I am more of an ambivert – needing time to myself to recover and rejuvenate. It was not diagnosed that I have dyslexia and dyspraxia until I was 26. However, as it was not diagnosed, I learned how to deal with it and apparently I am in the 98th centile for verbal reasoning – I could talk the hind legs off a donkey. The only way I could explain myself was by telling stories. However, I lost the confidence to do so over the years as a result of being bullied and spending years going through depression, anxiety and bulimia. Additionally, I actually found out while I am writing this book that I have ADHD. Better late than never!

When I was a little boy, I was bullied fairly relentlessly and my family was falling apart – mental illness, divorce, substance misuse. I viewed myself as 'the clumsy, fat, poor kid' and this has been hard to shake. When I was 18 and had next to no qualifications (having worked since age 13), I was told that I should get a trade – so I became an electrician.

When I was 20 and learned to walk again (after an accident that meant I couldn't walk for a year), I was told that I should get a job in a bank – so I became a cashier. When I was 23, I was told that I didn't have the grades or acumen for university – so I became a steel erector. I have worked as a hod carrier, sexual health adviser, bouncer. You name it, I have probably done it and in each job I was always told by others, 'you're doing great, this job will do'. In the seven years since finishing university, however, I have realized that I am capable of so much more and that you expand to the limits and story you impose on yourself, rather than accepting the narrative that others write for you.

After university I managed to get a dream job at a Big Four consultancy, where people spoke well and had been to good schools. I was slightly different, the former bouncer and electrical apprentice covered in tattoos. I tried my utmost to present myself like my peers and found common anxieties bubbling up. The reality is, you are never going to be able to be anyone else and we have to embrace ourselves, warts and all. This is far from easy to do, however, and we often accept the limitations that we and others put on ourselves – much easier to blend in.

I was told once by a manager that you can't be talking to people and be the showman all the time and to tone it down; another one told me to adopt a more 'professional' and less 'friendly' attitude; yet another told me to stop offering to make cups of tea for everyone. I took all this in. I guess I needed to be quiet, get in line and be like everyone else. I learned what is called a 'personal brand' that we are taught in the workplace. However, a personal brand is anything but personal; it is, rather, a curated version of what it is to be a 'professional'. Be yourself, just not too much. Authenticity please, but not that much.

I have tried and failed at being someone else for years. So I have given up. Now I turn up as myself every day and have unlearned the 'personal brand'. I may not be the most polished, subtle person you will encounter (understatement); rather a little clumsy, energetic and authentic. I only wear a mask once a year now on 31 October. I go as far as to say, this is the best thing I have ever done for myself and my well-being. You are never going to be anyone else, so why try? How can you embrace more of your authentic self today?

We are going to frame it in Joseph Campbell's hero's journey. This is the common narrative archetype, or story template, that involves a hero who goes on an adventure, learns a lesson, wins a victory with that newfound knowledge and then returns home transformed. The hero's journey can be boiled down to three essential stages:

The departure: The hero leaves the familiar world behind.

The initiation: The hero learns to navigate the unfamiliar world.

The return: The hero returns to the familiar world.

The hardships you have been through make you who you are and the hero's journey repeats again and again ad infinitum throughout our lives. Maybe you are currently going through something, or perhaps you are on your return as you read this chapter. The sooner you realize that all authentic heroes have been through something similar, the better. This is what makes your story worthwhile and what will separate you from the rest. Embrace it.

Tip 1: Appreciate the journey. Without the hardships, you would not be the resilient person that you are. Yes, it was tough, but you are stronger for it.

Tip 2: No two stories are the same. You can't compare apples to oranges. There is no one like you and I think that makes you pretty bloody special. Celebrate that fact and try your best to embrace it; when you welcome and embrace your story it will be your superpower.

Tip 3: Embrace the narrative. You probably wish that you didn't need to suffer as much as you have. We all feel that way. However, no story worth listening to is without pain and suffering. Harry Potter's parents didn't die, he went to Hogwarts, the end. Doesn't have the same ring to it, does it? This is how heroes are made.

Tip 4: Share your story. I was unable to tell anyone apart from my mum about my battle with bulimia for years; however, when I was finally able to share, it felt as if a massive weight had been lifted. Since then I have spoken to tens of thousands of people at events and millions on social media. It still hurts to think about it, to really think about it; however, because of what I went through, I will help millions of people and that is pretty amazing. Who knows, maybe you sharing what you have been through is just what someone needs to begin their own hero's journey.

I wish I could go back in time and have a word with that anxious, sad little boy. I would look into his eyes and tell him, 'It's cool, you tell you stories, you speak up, you are wonderful because you are different', and then I would give him a big old hug.

You are not as terrible as you think, and if you think everyone else has it sorted all the time, well. Take a minute today and remind yourself of what you have been through, all the good things you do, how you turn up and embrace who you are with open arms.

You are a hero, even if you don't realize it yet. You will.

Recently I was thinking, 'I would love a couple of sick days to just watch some rubbish on Netflix and relax. No emails, no calls, just switch off.' Careful what you wish for, because that opportunity presented itself for me this week and I was sick as a dog – fever, runny nose, cough, headache, the full package. Great. Could I keep myself from emails and social media, etc? Nope. I could not keep my hand out of the digital cookie jar. Just one peek won't hurt.

A lot of us take meaning from motion and performance and when we take away the motion, what happens to our meaning? It's like a game of musical chairs when the music stops. Jerry Colona said something on the Tim Ferriss podcast recently and it really resonated with me: 'Of course we want to play all the time, but sometimes we need to sit out to pause, rest and reflect and we will be back for the next game.' I feel you, Jerry.

I would rather do basically anything than relax. Anyone need their ironing or taxes done? Question time, ask yourself, when you are super busy, flat out, back to back, etc, are you able to work with enthusiasm, creativity and more importantly, are you happy? Do you think that you will be able to relax and find some joy in your day if you are glued to a screen for 13+ hours? I'm sure you are great at grinding out widgets and answering emails, but is this productive work or busy work? Do you think that if you have no free time, you will be able to come up with the answers and solutions for the challenges of tomorrow? Ok, you get it now, I'll stop asking questions.

We need to unpick the myth that more always equals more. A strong work ethic is something that we praise, but not enough is said of a strong rest ethic, which is equally, if not more important. Sure it's amazing that James and Zarah 'went above and beyond', working weekends to get the project done and over the line; admirable, even. Can someone wake them up please? They are dribbling on their desks. Or perhaps, it's a shame that they were unable to spend more than three minutes with their families over the past two weeks and this is not a one off, is it? Let's not kid ourselves. Would it not be amazing one day to hear that Cyrus hit the deadline, with happy clients, and did so without having to sacrifice his personal life? Remember, there is no such thing as work–life balance; if we try to balance life against work, work wins every time. Life first, work second. It's just life, of which work is one part.

I find it easy to put in the work, to do more, just like you! However, I find it much more difficult to just be, to switch off. How can I, when there is always more I can be doing? Also, if I'm honest with you, I don't feel like I deserve it. The rest that is. Who am I/you trying to prove something to? Have you ever got ahead of your inbox? I work in a large global organization; I could work 52 hours per day and I would still come back to emails and messages tomorrow.

Robert Pirsig, philosopher and author of *Zen and the Art of Motorcycle Maintenance*, noted that people need periods of doing nothing like plants need periods of darkness:

> If a plant gets nothing but sunlight it's very harmful. It has to have darkness too. In the sunlight, it converts carbon dioxide to

oxygen, but in the darkness, it takes the oxygen and converts it back into carbon dioxide. People are like that, too. We have to have some periods of doing and some periods of non-doing.[62]

I wish I could, but I can't share tips for what a rest ethic should look like, because it's different for everyone; some like to move, to be still, to be alone, to be with others, etc. For me, I prefer time alone, to be moving, progressive house music (no lyrics) and somewhere green. I have ADHD and the noise and external stimulus really helps me to relax. However, I know this is some form of a nightmare relaxation scenario for most of my family, colleagues and friends, who think that I'm a lunatic. As I write this, I'm listening to Fred Again's DJ set from Brixton – 10/10, would recommend.

I may not be able to share exactly what your rest ethic should look like, as everyone's will be different, unless you have a penchant for progressive house music, green spaces and some aggressive walking speed... Regardless, here's how you can develop and improve your work ethic.

Tip 1: The sweet spot. You can have too much or too little of everything. Working too much will burn you out and not enough will leave you languishing. Exercise too much and you are unable to sit on the toilet (leg day, am I right?), too little and you will atrophy. Spend too much time alone and you feel isolated, too little and you are socially fatigued. Have a think about your routines – what could you do more of and, more importantly, what could you do with a little less of?

Tip 2: You're allowed to rest. Give yourself permission to rest and prioritize it, like you do with your other commitments. Taking time off is not a sign of weakness or laziness, rather a necessary component to avoid becoming one of the burned-out masses. Do you think that LeBron James is lazy because he sleeps 12 hours per day (nine hours at night and a three-hour nap)? No, you don't, because he is the GOAT.

Tip 3: Schedule it in. Make rest a priority in your daily and weekly schedule. Just as you allocate time for work tasks and meetings, intentionally carve out dedicated periods for rest and rejuvenation. Treat these moments as non-negotiable appointments with yourself and honour them as you would any other commitment.

Tip 4: It doesn't have to be boring. Discover the activities and environments that help you relax and recharge; they do not have to be sedentary, contrary to popular opinion. Experiment with different approaches to rest; maybe you enjoy taking a midday yoga class, reading a book for an hour or going on a hike over the weekend. Whatever it is, the most important thing is that you enjoy doing it. If it's a chore, it won't last. I am not one to sit still for longer than eight seconds – you might be different. I feel most at peace when in the gym, but I'm weird.

Tip 5: Maintaining the path. Building a rest ethic takes time and effort. You will slip up sometimes, but don't give up! Keep reminding yourself of the importance of taking time off and why you established your rest ethic in the first place. If you are a data-driven person like me, tracking your behaviour will help keep you on track. If you treasure it, measure it. Plus, if all else fails, consider some negative incentives to keep you motivated. Maybe bet your friend or partner that you will clean the house or pay them money if you fall back into your old habits and find yourself responding to 'just one more email' at 8 pm when eating dinner with the family.

Tip 6: Nudge nudge. Put in place little reminders or nudges that encourage you to stick to your rest ethic; there are a gazillion apps for that. Maybe set a calendar reminder, post your guidelines on the fridge or get a buddy to help you stay on track. My best mate James is pretty good at keeping me on track: 'It's 9 pm, do you really need to respond to those comments now?' 'No James, I suppose I don't.'

That's it, I'm off to photosynthesize.

This is a two-part chapter: we are going to explore your own opinions and those of others.

Part 1: Your opinions

We all have that friend or family member who has a really strong opinion about everything. That person who seems to have some moral reaction to everything that is going on. If you are not sure who that is, I would take a peek in the mirror.

Our opinion takes objective situations and puts a label on them: ridiculous, amazing, unjust, devastating, etc. Opinion makes us poke our nosey little snout into situations where it is not needed. We find ourselves disagreeing with something Steve did during that meeting, or believing Lucy should have dealt with that client differently. Will your opinion change anything? Probably not. The mere notion of adopting a passive stance runs contrary to common opinion and is almost heretical. I realize this is not an easy thing to do, but just consider it.

It helps me to define whether a challenge or problem is a 'controllable' or an 'uncontrollable'. Controllables are things that I can control. They are in my sphere of influence. I can do something to affect the outcome. Examples include making a phone call, sending an email or scheduling a meeting. Uncontrollables are challenges or problems that I do not control. I can't ultimately control the outcome, as much as I wish it were different. Uncontrollables might include your landlord not renewing your lease, a storm shutting down the airport or the WiFi dropping while you're on an important call. There are myriad uncontrollables that you just can't influence. They are simply challenges that are externally determined.

If the challenge is a controllable, I'm able to take direct and prompt action; I'm able to influence the outcome. If the challenge is an uncontrollable, while still invested in the outcome, I adopt a more passive stance and simply monitor the outcome in the background. All I can do is my best regardless. I separate my actions from the outcome, understanding whether I can influence what comes to pass or not. If I do my best, I can be proud that is all I can do.

Getting frustrated or angry about something you can't change – an uncontrollable – is akin to holding a red-hot coal with the intent of throwing it at someone else, only you get burned. We should ask ourselves, can we do anything about the situation? If we can't, then it may be best to let it go and move on to more important things and get after those controllables.

Part 2: Others' opinions

It is absolutely natural to want to please the people around us, especially those we care about. However, we often waste our time and energy trying to please those who do not care or appreciate our efforts. This can be frustrating and demoralizing. To put it lightly.

It's important to remember that we can't please everyone, no matter how hard we try. Some people – family, friends, colleagues – are simply negative, unappreciative, threatened or they are going through something themselves and that is okay. They probably haven't read this book yet... We should focus on the people who appreciate us and our efforts and be positive in our interactions with them.

When we encounter people who are not receptive to our efforts, we shouldn't take it personally. It's not about us, it's about them. Keep being positive, focus on the people who appreciate you and when these people are good and ready you will be there. It is, however, important to recognize that there may be situations where we can't avoid working with or spending time with people who do not appreciate us.

For example, in a professional setting, we may need to work with difficult colleagues or superiors who don't acknowledge our hard work or contributions. 'Why doesn't everyone realize how great I am? I don't get it.' Additionally, in personal relationships, it may not always be feasible to simply cut ties with those who do not appreciate us. For example, we may have family members who are critical or unsupportive, but whom we still love. 'Yes, I love you, but I don't have to like you.' I have been on the receiving end of those words a few times. In these cases, it can be helpful to set boundaries and limit our exposure to said negativity, while also finding ways to appreciate and validate ourselves. You are doing what you can; you can't affect how Suzanne from Marketing reacts.

As Shane Parrish, author of the *Brain Food Blog*, wrote: 'Few things are more important in life than avoiding the wrong people... We unconsciously become what we're near. If you work for a jerk, sooner or later, you'll become one yourself.'[63]

How do we let go of those pesky opinions?

Tip 1: Be mindful of your opinions. Take a step back and think about why you hold a certain opinion. Think, where did that come from? Is it based on facts or emotions? Are you jumping to conclusions without fully understanding the situation? Check yourself before you wreck yourself.

Tip 2: Perspective is key. It's important to remember that everyone has different experiences and opinions. When engaging in discussions or debates, try to understand the other person's point of view. This can help you broaden your own perspective and may even lead to a better understanding of a certain situation. Even if they are horrendously wrong. 'Of course pineapple belongs on pizza.'

Tip 3: Let it go. As Elsa from *Frozen* once said, 'Let it go'. Holding onto opinions that do not serve you or getting angry about uncontrollables are one-way tickets to being miserable. Learn to let go of opinions that are causing you stress or anxiety, and focus on the things that matter, the things that you can change.

Tip 4: Don't take it personally. When someone disagrees with you or doesn't appreciate you, it can be easy to take it as a personal attack. However, it is important to remember that opinions are subjective and that everyone has the right to their own thoughts and beliefs. Try not to take it personally and instead focus on finding common ground or agreeing to disagree. Consider, too, that the person you are speaking with may be going through a hard time. Ask, 'How are you?' Then ask again, 'How are you really?'

Tip 5: Two ears one mouth. When engaging in discussions, make sure to actively listen to the other person. This means giving them your full attention and not interrupting or dismissing their thoughts or feelings. Sure, you think you're right and want to show them. But consider this – maybe you're not. Listen to what they have to say. Because, who knows, you might learn a thing or two. I need to heed my own advice better with this one.

If you were to ask my opinion on the matter (not that I have one), opinions are a part of life. However, they do not have to control us – yours or theirs. By limiting the number of opinions we hold and focusing on the things that we can control, we can live happier and more fulfilling lives. Similarly, by not worrying about pleasing everyone and focusing on the people who appreciate us, we can build stronger relationships and find more joy in the interactions that matter.

25
A LIFE FULL OF MISERY

There is a historical proverb that goes 'My life has been filled with terrible misfortune, most of which never happened.'

This isn't just a relatable saying, there's a study that proves it. This study looked into how many of our imagined calamities never actually come to be.[64] In this study, subjects were asked to write down their worries over an extended period of time and then identify which of their imagined misfortunes did not actually happen. Lo and behold, it turns out that 85 per cent of what subjects worried about never happened, and with the 15 per cent that did happen, 79 per cent of subjects discovered either that they could handle the difficulty better than expected, or the difficulty taught them a lesson worth learning. This means that 97 per cent of what you worry over is not much more than a fearful mind punishing you with exaggerations and misperceptions.

We are going to do this chapter a little differently together and you can do this activity alone, with friends, colleagues or loved ones; it doesn't take long and this perspective has been a game changer for me!

Reflection time. Go back to a time (12+ months ago) when a lot of your headspace was occupied by a specific worry. For example, a presentation, you said something you regret to a friend, you found out you need a new boiler, pressure to meet a deadline, etc. Really go back there and try and feel the worry again. I know it's uncomfortable, but try.

So, was the anticipation worse than the occurrence itself? What did you learn? Are you stronger as a result?

Step 1. Write down three things you are currently worried about: for example, a looming deadline, preparing for a presentation or a difficult conversation with a loved one. We are going to split them into controllables and uncontrollables, as we discussed in the last chapter. This is also known as the Stoic Dichotomy of Control. Epictetus, one of the fathers of the stoic school of philosophy, shared with us about 2,000 years ago that some things are within our power, while others are not. Within our power are opinion, motivation, desire, aversion and whatever is of our own doing. Not within our power are our body, our property, reputation, office and whatever is not of our own doing.[65]

Step 2: Circle what is under your control and underline what is outside your control.

Step 3: Do one thing this weekend to either advance a controllable or to mitigate an uncontrollable and put in time to reflect on how it went.

This is all we can ever do. Remember that.

Do you want to know the million-dollar question that I use to stop worry in its tracks? When we feel our mind running down the worry rabbit hole, let us pause and ask ourselves: 'Will this matter in a year?' Chances are it won't and if, in the small chance it does – 3 per cent likelihood – we deal with it.

Let's deal with the controllables and let the uncontrollables go, because as Mary Schmich once said, 'Worrying is like trying to solve an algebra equation by chewing gum.'[66] Easier said than done for sure, but we can try; also, has anyone got any gum?

The best time to plant a tree was 20 years ago. The second-best time is now.

CHINESE PROVERB

Are you waiting for the perfect moment to start something new? Are you waiting for when the project dies down to sign up to see a therapist, start your new diet, or take that leap of faith with that career change you have wanted for years? If so, you are most certainly not alone. I am a proud member of the serial procrastinator club; I'd do the secret handshake with you, but I was too busy to attend the session. Most of us face this problem in our lives where we keep waiting for the perfect moment to start something new: 'I'll start when…'. But what if I told you that waiting for the right moment is just a myth?

According to a 2022 study conducted by YouGov in the UK, 21 per cent of Britons set New Year's Resolutions; however, only 28 per cent stuck to all of theirs, 53 per cent kept some, 17 per cent didn't keep any of the resolutions they made and, laughably, 2 per cent were not able to remember: 'resolutions, what resolutions?'. Somewhat unsurprisingly, health resolutions dominated the top three, with saving more money coming in fourth.[67]

But that begs the question, why do we wait for these perfect moments? Are we not just ratcheting up the pressure by trying to do it all in one go? Oh, we do love to make it difficult for ourselves. We convince ourselves that we will start our new diet on January 1st and finally lose the love handles – 'Someone throw the Christmas chocolate out, please!' Sure, you are definitely going to start saving a bit more money once the kitchen has been renovated... ahh, maybe after the holiday to Skiathos, too. As you already know, there will never be a perfect moment.

The longer we wait, the harder it becomes to take that first step. We become more comfortable in our current situation, and change becomes more difficult. 'Sure, I could go running, but episode seven of the fifth season of *Modern Family* isn't going to watch itself, is it? I'll go tomorrow.'

Three years ago, I made a commitment to start writing, making videos, producing content and even applied for a TED talk. I told everyone who would listen that I would do a TED talk and I would write a book. Was I ready? Definitely not. Was I scared? Absolutely. But do I wish I'd started a day, week or year earlier? A hundred per cent. It took a lot of courage to take that first step. I felt very vulnerable, but I realized that there will never be a perfect moment. So, I took that leap of faith and got started. I am dyslexic and had never spoken alone on stage when I said and shared this with everyone. Pretty ridiculous, right?

What this did for my self-belief is beyond comprehension. I started to see myself as a writer and speaker. Doing the things that a writer and a speaker does. I have engaged millions of people and I will engage a billion people in the future of wellbeing. As I've already shared with you, at 19 I had a horrific rugby accident, no qualifications, no job, no prospects, no hope and wanted to end my life. Whether you think you can or you can't, you're probably right. This is that book and the TED talk happened in May 2023.

So, what's stopping you from taking that first step? Is it fear of failure, or the belief that you are not ready yet? The truth is, you don't have to be ready to start. The journey itself will help you learn and grow and I promise that you will be surprised at how much you can achieve if you start now. Year one, I engaged about 400,000 people; year two, 1.2 million; year three, 3.6 million and next year I think I will reach over 10 million people. Year five, I will reach 30 million people at the current rates of growth. Do I wish I'd started earlier? Yes. Am I hugely grateful that I just got going? Absolutely.

Here is another example – a health-related one, as we know this is the favourite every year. I recently decided to stop drinking. Being a British man from a working-class background, this was the longest I'd not had a drink since I was 14, when I started drinking cheap cider in the park with my friends. Good old British culture. At first I was thinking, what am I going to do, how am I going to socialize, relax, date, etc? I truly felt like I would never drink again, but I lasted five months before having another drink (which is a new record by three months). I will try again next year.

This period of not drinking saved me 188,000 empty calories, which is the same as 53 pounds of body fat or 24.41 kg for my imperial friends, and I dropped 5 per cent body fat. I now have a raving chocolate addition to deal with, but one thing at a time! I was also able to save over £2,500. That sounds like a crazy amount to spend on booze, but when you consider that a pint of beer can cost £8 in London, it soon adds up.

So, what have I learned from stopping a habit and starting a new one that could help you take that first step?

Tip 1: Role models. When quitting the beers, it really helped me to surround myself with some amazing teetotallers. The best part here is that you do not need to know your role models personally, you have access to the world's greatest humans via YouTube, podcasts, books, etc. I am supported by Rich Roll, Mark Manson and the amazing author Catharine Gray, whose book *The Unexpected Joy Of Being Sober* is a delight.

Tip 2: Little chunks. The late, great Desmond Tutu once said, 'There is only one way to eat an elephant: a bite at a time.' What he meant by this was, if the task at hand seems daunting and overwhelming, break it down into smaller, achievable goals. This will help you stay motivated and focused as you tick things off.

Tip 3: Visualization. Imagine how you will feel once you achieve your goal – live it, breathe it, smell it, taste it; be there and savour the moment. To really take this up a notch, put it out in the world and tell everyone that will listen.

Tip 3: Utilizing Parkinson's Law. Parkinson's Law is the adage that work will expand to fill the time allotted for its completion. To combat that, we need to visualize our goal, take our chunks and set a timeline to achieve these micro-goals. It doesn't seem so daunting now.

Tip 4: A data-led approach. If you want to lose weight, don't just think about how much you want to lose; try to collect some more data points to incentivize yourself, e.g. how much money you will save, body fat reduction, increased step goal, etc. The richer picture that you are able to paint, the more you will create a more compelling goal/plan for you to stick to!

Tip 5: Negative and positive reinforcement. Give yourself a pat on the back when you achieve your micro goals, maybe even a little present. On the flip side, as mentioned in Chapter 23, 'Rest ethic', you can also make little bets with friends/family. For example, if you don't hit your target, you have to wash the dishes or donate to a charity of their choice.

Tip 5: Social pressure. As mentioned in the visualization tip, by putting your future self out in the world, this will create some additional pressure for you to stick to your goals and achieve your ambitions. This one is not for the faint-hearted.

Remember, there will never be a perfect moment, nor will anyone give you the green light. So why not get started today? You got this.

BACK-TO-BACK-TO-BACK MEETINGS

Spoiler alert: back-to-back meetings result in increased stress on our brain and are not an efficient use of our time. Time for a game of 'would you rather' – and no, going into the closet with me is not an option. Scenario A: Five back-to-back video calls, no breaks, you are dying to go to the toilet and your to-do list is continuing to grow, so much so that it is now on another page – sounds fun, right? Or scenario B: You still have five meetings, but each ends 5–10 minutes early, you get up, stretch your legs, make a cup of coffee and sit by the window for a minute, before coming back to hear Nigel deliver his rousing, riveting, rapturous quarterly finance update – at least you had that coffee!

I think I know which one you chose. If you chose A, well, I'm not sure what to say – skip ahead to the next chapter. For the rest of you, we all know what we would rather do, but how often do you find yourself jumping from one meeting to another with no breaks in between? This is hardly surprising given the fact that according to Microsoft, we now have 250 per cent more meetings than we did pre-pandemic.[68] Well, at least we have less to do outside of those meetings… Oh wait, workload hasn't changed, if anything it's higher. Perfect. Many of us experience the brain-melting negative effects of back-to-back meetings and it's time to do something about it.

Don't worry, this chapter has something for you, even if you are lucky enough to not be one of those souls who has to spend their entire waking life in meetings every single day, on repeat, ad infinitum.

According to another recent Microsoft study, back-to-back meetings are not only stressful but can also be damaging to our brains.[69] The study used EEG caps (you know, the ones that look like shower caps, or the cap you used to peroxide your hair blond to look like Eminem back in 2007) to measure brain wave activity and stress detection in two groups of participants who sat through four meetings back to back. One group was given a 10-minute break in between each meeting, while the other was not.

The results were shocking but hardly surprising. The group who took breaks between meetings were able to reset their brain stress activity, while the other group experienced a distinct increase in stress (a higher level of beta waves – those associated with stress), which was actually compounded by jumping from one meeting to the next. The research highlighted three main things: breaks between meetings allow the brain to 'reset', reducing the cumulative build-up of stress across meetings; back-to-back meetings can decrease your ability to focus and engage; transitioning between meetings can be a source of high stress. Imagine this: it's 2.57 pm and I'm speaking to someone else at 3 pm and this meeting is nowhere near finished and here comes the inevitable anxiety.

If you think that you are productive after your ninth consecutive meeting, think again. There is a distinct difference between being busy and being productive and we have very much conflated the two. We are working longer than ever, with the average workday expanding by 13 per cent since March 2020; collaboration tools are ubiquitous.[70] However, according to the National Institute of Economic and Social

Research, the productivity (real GDP) growth rate in the UK averaged 0.5 per cent per annum from 2008–2020, compared to 2.3 per cent in the 34 years prior.[71] Of course, this is due to a whole host of reasons, but working longer with more meetings is not having the desired positive effect for us as individuals, organizations or societally. So why are we doing it?

We all know how it feels to be in back-to-back meetings without a break. It's like we are on a never-ending treadmill, constantly trying to catch up with ourselves. But what if we could change that? What if we could save time, reduce stress and be more productive all at the same time? The solution is rather simple: auto-schedule your meetings to finish 5–10 minutes early – this is **Tip 1**.

By auto-scheduling meetings to finish early, we allow our brains to reset, our stress to dissolve and we can actually save a lot of time – 4.8 work weeks per year actually (assuming six meetings per day and an average saving of 7.5 minutes). Crazy right? Now imagine a whole organization did this – 5,000 people × 4.8 work weeks = 24,000 work weeks saved, which is equivalent to hiring 500 new full-time staff.

Tip 2: Share the love. If someone keeps putting 30-minute/ one-hour meetings in your diary, share with them how to do it. It will take seconds and you will both benefit.

Tip 3: Intentionality. The quickest and best meetings are intentional: send an agenda, consider the attendants, no multitasking (I see you typing away), finish on time (this will drive focus), share outcomes ahead of time and, finally, decline meetings that do not have the above. People will soon start to include and consider them.

Tip 4: The meeting audit. Challenge yourself and your colleagues over the next two weeks to ruthlessly audit your calendars. The only audit you have and will ever want:

- Step 1: Go through your calendar and answer the following questions. If you answer no to any of them, please proceed to next step:
  - Does the meeting have clear objectives, agenda, outcomes, etc?
  - Does the meeting finish 5/10 minutes before the hour/half past?
  - Is the meeting within my working hours, e.g. not at lunch or before/after hours?
  - Am I a contributor, SME, approver/decision maker?
  - Will I be impacted by a resulting outcome?
  - Will reviewing the meeting minutes/action items not be sufficient?
  - Is my role in the meeting clear?
  - Am I the only person from my team attending?
- Step 2: Take one of the following courses of action:
  - Decline the invite
  - Reduce the frequency/cadence
  - Reduce the length
  - Suggest a different communication channel – teams, email, etc
  - Reduce/remove some of the attendants

- Ask for an updated agenda, objectives, expected outcomes
- Delete

We are not interfaces on machines (not yet, anyway) and shouldn't treat ourselves and others that way. Time to step away. The antidote to meeting overwhelm is simple: take short breaks. Revolutionary.

I have to go – I have another call to jump on.

28

JOMO

In June 2022 I was made redundant and had to spend my entire summer applying, interviewing, preparing for whatever was next. Additionally, I was still posting every single day on social media. I thought to myself, 'If people think "wellbeing", I want them to think of me and I have to keep showing up to make this happen, even if I don't want to.' I was probably putting in more hours when I was jobless than when I was working.

After three months on the hunt, I managed to land my dream job at Deloitte as the Future of Wellbeing Lead, helping governments and organizations around the world to develop wellbeing strategies that 'actually work', rather than the nonsense we normally see. As soon as I signed the contract, I felt as if a massive weight had been lifted from my shoulders. I am from a working-class background and money has always been a concern in my life. Until the contract was signed, I could not relax; there was always that voice in the back of my head saying, 'How are you going to pay the bills? Worry, worry, worry.' Soon as the ink dried on the contract, I booked a trip to Mexico to switch off before starting my new job.

Being the diligent influencer that I am (yes, I was a little bit sick in my mouth as I wrote that), I prepared, created and scheduled posts to go out daily while I was away travelling the Yucatán for two weeks. I said to myself that I would let them autopublish and not look. So, I deleted my social media apps to prevent myself from dipping into the digital cookie jar.

Could I stay away? Nope, of course I couldn't. I knew a post was going out at a certain time and I would look to see how it was going or see who messaged/emailed. I just could not shake the idea that I needed to stay connected, because if I didn't I would miss some life-changing opportunity. What if I'm asked to speak at X event, Y person has reached out or if I got the book deal? I was in one of the most beautiful places on earth, diving into cenotes, swimming in the Caribbean Sea, eating tacos and drinking margaritas; I had worked my butt off all summer to land a new job, I was shattered and deserved to switch off, right? I just could not help myself – what if I missed something?

Twelve days passed like this. 'Oh, just one more look.' Download, delete, download, delete and repeat. I thought to myself, 'You have two more days before you go back to inboxes, posts, comments, etc; if you don't switch off now, you never will.' I left my phone in the Airbnb and spent the entire day on one beach. I went out that night and left the phone again; I walked slowly to dinner listening to the waves caress the shore, sat and watched the other couples and families laugh and smile as I ate, I walked the long way home with my toes in the water and somewhere along the way my fear of missing out (FOMO) turned into the joy of missing out (JOMO). My phone battery died and I did not charge it again until I got to the airport.

You instinctively know this feeling; take a second to think about it. Maybe you're not on a Mexican beach, but you have been in this scenario and we are going to explore JOMO in a bit more detail together.

JOMO is all about embracing the idea of disconnecting from the constant hustle and bustle of modern life, and taking the time to reflect and reconnect with yourself and the people in your life that matter. It's all about understanding that it's okay to say no sometimes and that we simply do not have time to do everything, nor do we want to.

So why is JOMO so important? Well, for starters, FOMO is a real problem. Nearly 7 in 10 (69 per cent) of millennials experience FOMO, the most of any age group. Millennials are also the most likely to purposely try to create FOMO among their peers, with 33 per cent saying they have done so compared to 12 per cent of those in other age groups.[72] And it is definitely not just millennials – people of all ages and backgrounds fight with the FOMO monster on a regular basis. If you think you don't, pop open social media and have a scroll for five minutes – check out Chapter 46, 'David vs Goliath: social media', for more of this.

However, we do not just experience FOMO when we are missing BBQs, parties, holidays, etc, but also with regard to meetings, deadlines and grading papers; according to LinkedIn, 70 per cent of professionals admit that even when they do take vacation, they don't break away. The number one reason? Fifty-six per cent say that they don't want to fall behind.[73]

LinkedIn also shared that a lot of people only step away from work in the first place to pursue a side hustle (which of course is admirable and is actually what I am doing today by writing this book). More than 70 per cent of professionals now have a side hustle outside of their primary job, and of these professionals, 40 per cent are using holiday days to work on their passion project.

Why do we do this to ourselves? I understand the need to work and earn enough money to survive, but for the people fortunate enough to have reached a position where we don't have to worry about paying the electric bill next month, we continue to plug ourselves back in willingly. A lot of us are living to work, rather than working to live, and we do it voluntarily. I'm as bad as you are here, so I'm not casting judgement. Is everything going to come tumbling down because you went to Budapest for a long weekend? If the answer is yes, then you have bigger things to worry about.

Trying to keep up with everyone else can be exhausting, and it can and will take a toll on our mental health. JOMO, on the other hand, can be incredibly refreshing. It allows us to take a step back, breathe and focus on the things that truly matter to us. Of course, embracing JOMO is not always easy. It can be hard to say no to things that we feel like we 'should' be doing, or to resist the pull of social media. But with a little practice, it's possible to make JOMO a part of our daily lives.

So how can we start embracing JOMO? Here are a few tips:

Tip 1: Set an example. Sixty-seven per cent of people say they would contact a colleague about work-related matters while the colleague is on holiday.[74] Don't be that person, because soon you will be on leave and you will wish you hadn't. So think twice before hitting send.

Tip 2: Single tasking. Multitasking is a myth; we single task but just switch between tasks constantly (some people are the exception to this rule, but I'm not and nor are you). Schedule something that is important to you and only do that one thing – no phones, no distractions, single tasking.

Tip 3: The present of presence. The past is history, the future is a mystery and the present is a gift. Be where you are right now; you will never be here again.

Tip 4: The definite yes. It's wise counsel to exercise caution before committing yourself to anything. Try to avoid making impulsive decisions, as your time, energy and resources are at stake. Take your time in responding to any requests, particularly when under pressure to make a quick decision. Consider defaulting to a 'no' response and only agree once you have had ample opportunity to thoroughly evaluate the situation and arrive at a well-informed and wise decision. If your answer is not a definite yes, then it should be a no.

Tip 5: Celebrate your downtime. It's easy to feel like we are wasting time when we are not doing anything 'productive'. But the truth is, downtime is as important as any moment of productivity, as we discussed in Chapter 23, 'Rest ethic'. So the next time you find yourself with some free time, try to embrace it rather than feeling guilty about it – you deserve it.

Who wants a taco?

29

SOLITUDE

Do you associate solitude with positive or negative feelings? 'True solitude – as opposed to the failed solitude we call loneliness – is a fertile state, yet one we have a hard time accessing.'[75] We have notifications and invitations coming out of our ears for either in-person events or digital connection; this can feel like we are constantly connected with people either physically or digitally. In today's hyperconnected world, it can be challenging to consider solitude or even a moment alone. It's difficult to decline invitations without feeling guilty or telling a little white lie. We often feel compelled to attend social events or stay connected digitally – hello again, FOMO.

For the majority of my life, I considered myself a complete extrovert, someone who needed to be around people all of the time, someone who could not spend time alone. There was a reason for that though (well, there were many, but I'll save that for counselling) – it was because I had never tried to spend time alone. I thought so little of myself growing up and for most of my adult life, I looked for validation completely externally, as a lot of us do. I needed to be patted on the back, to be compensated, to win awards, do crazy challenges (cycle the UK, pull double-decker buses, walk across countries). It didn't matter what I thought about myself, only what others said. Over the years as I have worked on myself,

I have unlearned the need to please everyone and be liked by all in order to feel a sense of worth. Through this process, I've discovered that I'm more of an ambivert – someone who displays both introverted and extroverted tendencies. Most of us are. It's not easy to bucket people into two camps, which is what we tend to do – I am X or I am Y and consequently need Z; life is not that simple and neither are you. Sorry, I don't mean to be assertive and bold, it must be the fact that I'm a Leo...

Since my discovery, I have learned that there are different types of ambiverts. According to Dr Domina Petric there are three:

- outgoing introverts: introverts who can be outgoing in certain situations, around certain people or when they absolutely need to be;
- antisocial extroverts: extroverts who need time to recharge before socializing or who like to be alone more than a typical extrovert;
- social introverts: introverts who can behave in a more extroverted way when needed.[76]

I associate most with the antisocial extrovert, which I quite like. Maybe I'm just getting old and cranky, who knows? But what I do know is that solitude has become as important for me as regular exercise.

Fyodor Dostoevsky captures it perfectly: 'Solitude for the mind is as essential as food is for the body.'

Shane Parish wrote:

Loneliness has more to do with our perceptions than how much company we have. It's just as possible to be painfully lonely surrounded by people as it is to be content with little social contact. Some people need extended periods of time alone to recharge, others would rather give themselves electric shocks than spend a few minutes with their thoughts.[77]

Strap me in, Shane.

Are you ever surrounded by people but still feel lonely? Do you find it difficult to spend time alone without feeling anxious or uncomfortable? If so, you might be in need of some solitude. Solitude is a state of being alone without being lonely. It's a chance to reflect and to be in touch with your inner self. In today's world, as we have discussed throughout the book, we are constantly connected to technology, making us feel that we are surrounded by people constantly. We need to recognize that our online connections can be superficial and fleeting, fast food for the brain. It may be filling, but it will not provide the nourishment and sustenance that we need to thrive. The ubiquitous, shallow, rapid connections actually cause loneliness, loneliness being juxtaposed to solitude, which is a fertile state – so how do we go about cultivating it?

Solitude functions like the equalization of pressure in a confined space. If we are constantly exposed to action and anxiety, our inner distractions and tensions have no outlet. They accumulate inside us and amplify with each passing day. Although we can distract ourselves temporarily, eventually they will reach a boiling point, figuratively speaking. Our stress levels surge, and we may unintentionally direct our anxiety towards others. In extreme cases, we lose control and create chaos. Conversely, when we quiet the external environment and spend quality time alone, the surrounding pressure begins to diminish. It provides space for our stress, uncertainty and struggles to gradually release and fill the newly created 'emptied' space around us.

Even those in positions of power recognize the importance of solitude despite their busy schedules. During WWII, Dwight Eisenhower took regular trips to a secluded cottage where he would walk, play bridge and golf, and where any mention of 'work' was forbidden. At the same time, thousands of miles over the Atlantic, during the height of the war and the Blitz, Winston Churchill was soaking in baths for hours on end, spending his free time painting and bricklaying (each to their own, I guess). Admittedly the world was very different in the 1940s... but you get me.

For a modern example, let's take Bill Gates. He should have a fairly good grasp on the digital world in which we find ourselves. Bill Gates still takes one week twice a year and escapes by himself to a secret wooden cabin somewhere in a cedar forest in the Pacific Northwest. It's what he calls his 'Think Week'. Gates arrives by helicopter or sea-plane and spends the week reading papers. He reads as many papers as possible, sometimes doing so for 18 hours a day, staying up until the wee hours of the morning. Work done during one of his Think Weeks eventually led to the launch of Internet Explorer in 1995.[78] Still not convinced?

OK, so you don't have time or resources to take yourself off to a remote cabin for weeks on end, I get that. Are we able to create a bit of space for solitude each day? Let us ask the executive chairman and former CEO of LinkedIn, Jeff Weiner. Just imagine how many people are asking for his help, time, expertise, opinion. The thought of it makes me anxious. Also consider being the person responsible for ensuring that thousands of people are led effectively, that they are doing meaningful work and also get paid each month. To top all that, the reputation of the business depends on you and your ability to lead – make any bad decisions and you are publicly shamed. Sounds pretty exhausting, right?

Despite the constant demands and pressures, Weiner deliberately schedules at least 90 minutes each day to do nothing:

> In aggregate, I schedule between 90 minutes and two hours of these buffers every day (broken down into 30- to 90-minute blocks). Above all else, the most important reason to schedule buffers is to just catch your breath. There is no faster way to feel as though your day is not your own, and that you are no longer in control, than scheduling meetings back to back from the minute you arrive at the office until the moment you leave. I've felt the effects of this and seen it with colleagues. Not only is it not fun to feel this way, it's not sustainable.[79]

So how do you start cultivating some solitude in your life?

Tip 1: Pockets of solitude. One way is to set aside a regular time each day for yourself, even if it's just 10 minutes. You can use this time to meditate, journal, take a walk or just sit quietly and breathe.

Tip 2: Unplug. If you leave your phone and laptop at home, you are now uncontactable. Don't go too far as you might get lost, but a lap of the park untethered can be incredibly liberating.

Tip 3: Take your headphones out. I have my AirPods in nearly all the time. I now challenge myself to go for a walk or get on the metro without them and just be.

It can and probably will take a little bit of work before solitude turns into a pleasant experience. But once it does, it becomes maybe the most important relationship anybody ever has, the relationship you have with yourself. Whether you are an introvert, an extrovert, an ambivert or even if your name is Bert, don't be afraid to embrace solitude and make it a regular part of your life. If I can, you definitely can. As Jean-Paul Sartre cheekily once said, 'If you're lonely when you're alone, you're in bad company.' So spend some time alone, get to know yourself, and enjoy the benefits of solitude.

Sorry, I can't come tonight.

30

YOUR CIRCLE

It is no secret that the people we surround ourselves with can have a huge impact on our lives. From shaping our habits to influencing our decisions, the company we keep can either propel us towards success or hold us back. That is why Jim Rohn's quote, 'You are the average of the five people you spend the most time with', has become so popular. As this book is about wellbeing, we are going to consider this with a wellbeing lens: it is my belief that your mood, your health, your fitness, etc will also be an average of those five same people. Look around you and see for yourself. Does that mean we are stuck and are destined to become the average of the five people in our immediate vicinity? Which if you think about it is probably your manager, a colleague, your partner, a friend and maybe a family member. What a frightening thought. Imagine Frankenstein's monster with less patience, a weird sense of humour, road rage and a few extra pounds.

The good news here is that you do not necessarily have to know your role models personally in order to benefit from their wisdom and guidance. Back in 1930, Napoleon Hill suggested creating an imaginary council and consulting with them regularly. Hill himself would have breakfast with the likes of Edison, Carnegie and Napoleon every morning. Must have been some interesting conversations happening at that table. While we may not be able to have breakfast with our role models, we can still surround ourselves with their ideas and insights.

Thanks to the internet and social media, we now have access to an endless supply of information and inspiration from some of the most successful people in the world and the greatest minds from history. You have more information at your fingertips than any human has had in the history of humankind. Podcasts, books, blogs – these are all great ways to invite the world's best into your life. So, who will you invite into your club?

Mary Schmich's address to the Class of '97 in the *Chicago Tribune* captures it perfectly: 'Be careful whose advice you buy, but be patient with those who supply it. Advice is a form of nostalgia. Dispensing it is a way of fishing the past from the disposal, wiping it off, painting over the ugly parts and recycling it for more than it's worth.'[80] Told you I would return to this speech a few times.

This may sound rather grandiose, but I truly believe that podcasts and books completely changed my mindset and opened up my world. I was never a big reader growing up; I was dyslexic but wasn't diagnosed until I was 23. Hardly surprising that I didn't take to reading. It was also around this time that I began to listen to podcasts and audiobooks. I started with one or two episodes of Lewis Howes' *School of Greatness* and *The Tim Ferriss Show* and before I knew what was going on I was listening to their entire back catalogue of 500+ episodes in every free moment that I had. Their perspective and the perspective of the people they interviewed opened up my world and began to make me feel like I was capable of so much more, more than I could have ever dreamed. I was born to be a tradesman, until I realized I could do whatever I wanted (not that anything is wrong with being a tradesman; I would probably own a house by now if I was).

Charlie Munger, billionaire and right-hand man of Warren Buffet, said:

> In my whole life, I have known no wise people who didn't read all the time – none, zero. You'd be amazed at how much Warren Buffet reads – and at how much I read. My children laugh at me. They think I'm a book with a couple of legs sticking out. I can say personally that when I started to read seriously, my life changed for the better. I learned from the greatest minds that have ever been and believed I was capable of more for the first time in my life.[81]

You don't even need to read if you don't want to; you can listen, watch, stream.

And don't be afraid to think outside the box. Your role models and breakfast guests don't have to be traditional success stories; they can be anyone who inspires you to be a better version of yourself. Maybe it is a teacher who encouraged you to pursue your passions, or a friend who always lifts your spirits. Mum gets the odd invite to breakfast, as does Grandad. The key is to surround yourself with people who uplift and motivate you. I have never met Tim Ferriss personally, but I normally listen to him for two or three hours per week and I have read all of his books. I choose to consume content that is going to enrich me, to teach me, to lift me up, rather than doom scrolling for hours on end.

Derek Sivers takes a similar approach which I think is pretty cool:

> I have three mentors. When I am stuck on a problem and need their help, I take the time to write a good description of my dilemma, before reaching out to them. I summarize the context,

the problem, my options, and thoughts on each. I make it as succinct as possible so as not to waste their time.

Before sending it, I try to predict what they will say. Then I go back and update what I wrote to address these obvious points in advance. Finally, I try again to predict what they will say to this, based on what they have said in the past and what I know of their philosophy. Then, after this whole process, I realize I don't need to bother them because the answer is now clear.

If anything, I might email to thank them for their continued inspiration. Truth is, I have hardly talked with my mentors in years. None of them know they are my mentors. And one doesn't know I exist.[82]

So, what are some practical ways to invite the right people into your life?

Tip 1: Entry criteria. First and foremost, start by identifying the areas in your life where you want to improve. Whether it is your career, your relationships, your health or your personal growth, there are likely role models out there who have already achieved what you are striving for.

Tip 2: Search time. Look for podcasts, books, videos and blogs that speak to those areas specifically where you want to develop and surround yourself with them.

Tip 3: Not on the list. I used to work as a bouncer and would often have to tell people, 'Sorry, your name's not on the list, you're not allowed to come in.' Consider who you are not inviting and place me on the door of your imaginary breakfast. I will do it for free, too. There are a few people I love with all my heart, but I do not want to adopt their habits, mindset or diet, etc, and I could live without their advice. Sorry, no breakfast for you.

You may not know Arnold Schwarzenegger personally or be on first-name terms with the Dalai Lama, but that doesn't mean we are not able to surround ourselves with their ideas and insights. Thanks to the wonders of technology, ever since the invention of the printing press we can now invite the world's best into our lives whenever, wherever and however we want. So, who will you invite into your club? And perhaps more importantly, who are you not inviting, remembering that your wellbeing is an average of the five people you spend the most time with?

I'm off for breakfast – 'Of course I want an extra sausage'.

FRESH AIR

Pop quiz: what do you do to energize yourself? If you are anything like me, you probably reach for a cup of coffee, or six, and, in particularly dire circumstances, an energy drink. I mean, how else are we supposed to power through our never-ending list of tasks and responsibilities? But what if I told you that there was a simpler, more natural way to feel rejuvenated, revitalized and refreshed? And, may I add, legally. You will not get in trouble for bringing this back from South America – although it may be difficult to carry. What if I told you that all you need to do is step outside and breathe in some fresh air?

Now, I know what you are thinking: 'Fresh air? Come on, Ryan, that's not going to do anything for me, I'm shattered and have slept for 3.7 hours this year.' But hear me out. One study shows that being outdoors, getting some fresh air and being surrounded by nature, can improve energy by up to 90 per cent![83] That's right, 90 per cent. And it's not just a placebo effect either; there are real, tangible benefits to getting some fresh air.

For starters, breathing in fresh air can help clean out our lungs and improve our respiratory function. After all, when we are cooped up indoors all day, with the temperature never dropping below 21 or above 23 degrees centigrade, and we are constantly inhaling recycled air that is full of dust, allergens, pollutants and everyone's dead skin. Tasty. But when we step outside and take a deep breath, we are giving our lungs a chance to flush out all that gunk and replace it with clean, oxygen-rich air – depending on your city, of course. You may have to walk a bit to find it in London, New York or New Delhi.

But the benefits of fresh air do not stop there. The same study shows that a few big lungfuls can boost our mood, reduce stress and anxiety, and even improve our cognitive function. So the next time you are feeling frazzled or over-whelmed – which is probably right now – take this book with you and step outside for a few minutes and take in your surroundings. You might be surprised at how much better you feel afterwards. A bit rich really, given that I am writing this chapter on a flight to Hamburg, breathing in a cocktail of second-hand flatulence and body odour, but there you go.

Florence Nightingale knew about the power of fresh air, a long time before any scientific studies: 'It is the unqualified result of all my experience with the sick, that second only to their need of fresh air is their need of light.' Yeah, I would have felt like that too if I found myself in a late-19th-century hospital when cigarettes were prescribed for asthma, you may have been given a milk transfusion and you were lucky to make it to 40 years old. Yeah, I will go for a walk, thanks. Maybe this is where the saying 'walk it off' came from.

Of course, it's not always easy to find the time or motiva-tion to get outside, especially if you live in a city like I do. I don't step out of my front door into green meadows or sandy beaches and I have a busy schedule with very limited free time. But do not fret, my friend, there are plenty of ways to incorporate fresh air into your daily routine:

Tip 1: Round the block. Block it out in your diary and take a walk around the block. If you do not prioritize it, no one else will. One of the busiest people I know does this every single day. He says, if you want me between 12.30 and 1 pm, you will have to call me. I like that.

Tip 2: Crack a window. If you do not have time to get out today, as your manager has dropped a massive amount of work on your desk, classic. If this happens, you can crack open a window and let the air come to you. It's smart like that.

Tip 3: The bookend. You can make it a point to spend some time outside every morning or evening, before you start work and as soon as you finish. This can be in the form of a walk, a jog or simply sitting on your front step with a cup of tea.

Tip 4: The outside office. As we discussed in Chapter 1, 'Taking a stroll', if you are able to, take a call while outside having a walk – check the weather first. Or perhaps, if you have a chair and a table outside, why not migrate out there for the day? A cardboard box around the laptop works wonders, trust me.

And if you are still not convinced, just think about all the things you are missing – the changing of the seasons, the sound of birds chirping, the feeling of sunshine on your face... there is so much beauty and wonder to be found in the natural world, if only we take the time to appreciate it. See more in Chapter 21, 'Cosmic insignificance therapy'.

So the next time you're feeling tired, stressed or just in need of a pick-me-up, try not to reach for that cup of coffee just yet. Take a few minutes to step outside, breathe in some fresh air and let nature work its magic. Your body and mind will thank you for it. Or do both, I probably will...

32
COLD THERAPY

From the World's Strongest and Europe's Strongest Men (who are also brothers, Tom and Luke Stoltman) to Fearne Cotton and Joe Rogan, it seems that everyone on Instagram is diving into the sea in the depths of winter, jumping into ice baths or voluntarily turning the shower cold. Yes, I am one of those masochists. But why on earth would anyone subject themselves to such freezing torture? Cold therapy has gained popularity for its numerous health benefits – not just for looking cool on Instagram.

But some people take it even further, quite a bit further in fact, people like Josef Koeberl, an ice swimmer from Austria. Josef started with small steps, gradually increasing the time he spent in the ice-cold water. He has held several world records, including the longest time spent submerged in ice, which is an incredible two hours and 30 minutes – beating the record previously held by Wim Hof. The record has since been taken, but Josef told me (from a freezer in his garage, while I interviewed him for my show *The Audacious Goals Club*) that he intends to take the record back and break three hours. While most of us may not be able to or want to handle such extreme cold, Josef's story is a reminder of how powerful the human body can be. It can adapt and even thrive in extreme conditions.

But you don't have to break world records or travel to Austrian glaciers to experience the benefits of cold therapy.

Even simple practices like turning the shower cold or taking a dip in an ice bath can have significant health benefits, both physical and mental.

Let us start with the physical benefits, which are numerous. Cold exposure has been shown to increase metabolism and fat burning, which can aid in weight loss and weight management. It also boosts the immune system, improving your body's ability to fight off infections and diseases. Cold therapy can even reduce inflammation, relieve muscle soreness and promote faster recovery after intense exercise or injuries. Of course, there are pros and cons for everything – you'll just have to try for yourself and see how you feel.[84]

But it doesn't stop there. Cold showers or immersions can also have a positive impact on your mental health. Studies have shown that cold water exposure releases endorphins, those delightful little chemicals that make you feel good. It can boost your mood, reduce stress levels and maybe even alleviate symptoms of depression. So, by subjecting yourself to a chilly experience, you are giving your mental health a little boost, too.[85]

But here is the real juicy bit and the part that makes the most sense to me: cold therapy has been shown to improve your tolerance to stress. According to a 2022 study at the University of Bayreuth, by exposing yourself to the cold, you are actually training your body to adapt to challenging situations more effectively and this resilience can spill over into other areas of your life, helping you cope with everyday stressors and become more mentally and emotionally robust.[86] It does for me, anyway.

If you are ready to take the plunge, here are a few tips to get you started in the shower:

Tip 1: Start cold. Crank the dial to the left and start the water cold; try and do it after exercise if possible. Your body is already warm, and the contrast of cold water will feel even more invigorating. I shared this with a few people recently and they said I was a madman and they prefer to start warm. Do whatever works for you!

Tip 2: Hands first. Begin by submerging your hands in cold water for at least 10 seconds. Use this time to have a little pep talk with yourself. Repeat a mantra like 'YOU GOT THIS' and summon your inner courage. Let's go.

Tip 3: Go time. Take the leap and fully immerse your body in the cold water. Embrace the sensation and let it awaken your senses, because it will. You can even imagine you are walking on hot sand and doing a little victory dance – pirouettes are strongly encouraged.

Tip 4: Make noise. As you embrace the cold, let out some weird noises: 'he ho ha he he he ha'. Just be sure to give your flatmate, partner or kids warning beforehand. You would not want to alarm them unnecessarily – they may think there is some funny business going on.

Tip 5: Timebox the cold. Start with a short duration and gradually increase it over time. Once you are wet, lather up, rinse off, and then reward yourself with a turn of the dial to hot water. Ah, the sweet sensation of warmth, it feels soooo good.

But let us not forget about the legendary 'Iceman' himself, Wim Hof. His method combines cold exposure with specific breathing techniques and meditation to unlock the full potential of cold therapy. Through his extraordinary feats, Wim Hof has shown us that the human body is capable of incredible things when pushed to its limits, and you are capable of extraordinary things too. A couple of amazing examples of Wim's achievements are climbing Mount Kilimanjaro in shorts and running a half marathon above the Arctic Circle barefoot.

Now, I must confess that I have personally embarked on this chilly journey and the results have been pretty remarkable from a mental perspective. I feel much more resilient, as if the trials and tribulations that used to induce anxiety and stress simply wash over me, like a stone on the riverbed, impervious to the torrent raging above. Once you have taken an ice-cold shower first thing, everything that comes after just does not seem that difficult. A tricky email, awkward call, rubbish weather, cancelled trains – 'Meh, that's nothing, I'm an Iceman.' Equally, I have not been ill since I started – I know this is hardly a scientific study, but I'll take it! Lastly, another benefit I forgot to share is that you will spend much less time in the shower, therefore this is a productivity hack too. Result.

But don't just take my word for it. Give it a try and see how it affects your own life. Start small, be consistent, and gradually increase your exposure to the cold. Remember, discomfort is temporary, but the benefits can be long-lasting. And who knows, you might just discover a hidden power within yourself, just like the Iceman himself (Wim Hof or Josef Koeberl, not me – I'm more of a Slightly Cold Man).

I know you're now ready to take the plunge into the world of cold therapy (or you are at least considering it). Time to join the ranks of the icy masochists and embrace the exhilarating benefits of the cold.

Ah, sleep. The magical state of blissful slumber where dreams come alive and tiredness melts away. Well, at least that's how I have heard it should be. Nowadays, sleep has become a rather rare and elusive creature. We live in a society that glorifies busyness and praises those who burn the midnight oil. We wear our sleep deprivation like a badge of honour, proudly boasting about how little shut-eye we can survive on. But let me tell you a little well-known secret: lack of sleep is slowly but surely sucking the life out of us. As much as you think that you can survive on five or six hours' sleep (like Elon Musk claims he does), well you just can't. When was the last time you didn't feel tired?

Enter Matthew Walker, the modern-day Sandman and author of the eye-opening book (yes, I did mean that) *Why We Sleep*.[87] In his book, Walker unveils the science behind sleep and exposes the dire consequences of neglecting this vital aspect of our lives. And trust me, it's not pretty. Did you know that a staggering 35 per cent of adults don't get the recommended seven hours of sleep per night? That is a third of the population wandering through life in a zombie-like state, fuelled by caffeine, Skittles and sheer willpower in a perpetual state of yawning and red-eyedness.

But the consequences of sleep deprivation go far beyond feeling groggy and irritable, which is a state we all know far too well. Lack of sleep has been linked to a smorgasbord of health issues, including obesity, diabetes, cardiovascular disease and even a weakened immune system. In fact, a study from Warwick University found that consistently sleeping less than six hours per night increases the risk of premature death by 12 per cent.[88] Damn, time for bed.

Now, I do not mean to scare you, but the Sandman's warning is clear: prioritize your sleep now or pay the price later. Fortunately, there are practical solutions to rescue us from the ruinous clutches of sleep deprivation and restore our natural sleep rhythms, so we can sleep like a baby once more – so that is where that comes from. And no, I'm not talking about counting sheep, valium or a few glasses of wine to 'take the edge off'.

One of the most important factors is establishing a consistent sleep routine. Our bodies crave regularity, so try to go to bed and wake up at the same time every day, even on weekends. Yes, I know it's tempting to go out Friday and Saturday night, have one too many drinks and/or stay up binge watching Ted Lasso, but your body and mind will thank you for sticking to a schedule. I used to be a demon for it. I would go to bed at 10.30 Sunday to Thursday and 2–3 am Friday and Saturday after quite a few drinks. No wonder I was always tired. It may sound boring, but I tell you what is boring – being constantly tired. I tell you what is not boring – feeling energized and awake.

But wait, there is so much more. Did you know that the environment in which you sleep makes a world of difference? Your bedroom should be a sleep sanctuary, a cosy haven where relaxation reigns supreme (or something else, but we are not here to talk about that – maybe that can be my next book). Make sure the room is cool, dark and quiet. Banish electronic devices from the sacred sleep space, charge them away from you and put them on do not disturb and opt for a good old-fashioned book instead. You know, one of the ones made out of paper, with the pages. Trust me, your dreams will thank you.

Time for a nap. Yes, you heard me right, napping. It turns out that a well-timed nap can be a secret weapon in the battle against sleep deprivation. Studies have shown that a short power nap of around 20 minutes can boost alertness, enhance creativity and improve overall cognitive performance.[89] So, if you find your head dropped and those eyelids getting a bit heavy while in your sixth meeting of the day, if you are able to, relax into the embrace of the siesta. A few years ago, I worked in Argentina for a few months on a farm and we napped every day. I am not sure I have ever felt so happy, relaxed and energized. Surprising really, given the amount of Malbec we washed down every night.

Now, here is a little anecdote from my own sleep journey. I used to be a night owl, burning the midnight oil and wearing my sleep deprivation as a badge of honour. 'I only need six hours.' Oh, how misinformed and naive I was. After reading Walker's book, I decided that it was time to up my sleep game. I eat well, I train, I stretch, do XYZ to look after myself and I was still feeling sluggish and sleepy. I knew I needed to step it up. I created a bedtime routine that involved winding down at the same time every day with a good book, dimming the lights and banishing screens from my bedroom. Also, eliminating caffeine after 2 pm and cutting out the booze. The result? A rather miraculous transformation. I have gone from 17 slaps to the undeserving alarm clock before dragging myself out of bed at 7.45, to getting up at 6 am every day feeling energized and ready to go.

Time to address the big, bright, blue elephant in the room: the allure of late-night Disney+ binges and scrolling through social media feeds. We have all been there, lured into the digital abyss when we should be snoozing peacefully. Just one more episode of *Family Guy* won't hurt. Blink and it's 2 am. *Not again.* The blue light emitted by our screens wreaks havoc on our sleep hormones, disrupting our natural circadian rhythm. So, my sleepy friends, if we want to sleep, we need to put our devices to sleep before us. Consider implementing a technology curfew, shutting down electronic devices at least an hour before hitting the hay.

And speaking of blue light, let us talk about the power of natural light – we want this one. Our bodies are wired to sync with the natural rhythm of daylight, so make an effort to expose yourself to bright light in the morning – see Chapter 17, 'Hygge'. Throw open those curtains, step outside for a walk or simply bask in the sunlight streaming through your windows (wishful thinking in London). Your internal clock will thank you, and you will find yourself dozing off more easily when bedtime rolls around later. So, limit blue light, maximize natural light. Easy peasy.

Now, I must confess, I am no sleep expert like Matthew Walker. But his book has opened my eyes to the incredible superpower that is sleep. It is not a luxury or a nice-to-have, rather a necessity for our physical and mental wellbeing. Time to stop venerating and celebrating those who regularly pull all-nighters and survive on caffeine fumes, like this is something to aspire to.

Arianna Huffington used to be a burner of the midnight oil, subscribing to a very flawed definition of success, buying into the collective delusion that burnout is the necessary price we must pay. Then, in 2007, she had a painful wake-up call: she fainted from sleep deprivation and exhaustion, hit her head on her desk and broke her cheekbone. She wrote about this experience in *Thrive* and how she has changed her life to focus on her wellbeing, specifically her sleep first and foremost, becoming a bit of a sleep evangelist (her own words) in the process. Anyway, it's time to wrap this up – it's time for bed.

Arianna likes to take a hot bath with Epsom salts before bed, and I am a big fan of this one too. The hotter the better. I want to come out steaming and then sit on the balcony to cool down before going to bed. Aim to keep your bedroom between 60 and 67 degrees Fahrenheit or 15–19 degrees Celsius and you will slip into slumber quicker than a 'zzzzz' – that's **Tip 1.**

Tip 2: Avoid\limit afternoon caffeine. I would drink coffee until the second I went to sleep if I could. However, if I have caffeine after 2 pm I really struggle to sleep. I have made the switch to decaffeinated tea in the afternoon and I find that I am not wide awake when I hit the pillow anymore. We all have different tolerances to caffeine; my mum can drink coffee while brushing her teeth before bed, which I find slightly insane. The general consensus between the sleep experts is to not consume caffeine after 2 pm. Stick to that rule and you can't go far wrong.

Tip 3: The sleep routine. Our bodies crave regularity, so set a consistent bedtime and wake-up time. Yes, even on weekends. Of course, this is not doable all the time and you will break this rule, you party animal you, but do try to do it as much as you can – your eyelids will thank you.

Tip 4: The sleep sanctuary. Transform your bedroom into a sanctuary of sleep. Keep the room cool, dark and quiet.

Banish electronic devices from your sleep space, opting for a good old-fashioned book instead. Your bedroom is for two things and two things only.

Tip 5: The technology curfew. The allure of late-night digital distractions will wreak havoc on your sleep. Blue light emitted by screens disrupts your natural circadian rhythm. Establish a technology curfew, disconnecting from electronic devices at least an hour before bedtime and leaving them in another room if possible. Treat yourself to an old-school alarm clock. Your sleep hormones will thank you.

Tip 6: Natural light exposure. Our internal clock syncs with the natural rhythm of daylight. Expose yourself to bright light in the morning by opening curtains, going for a walk or simply basking in the sunlight where possible (use a SAD lamp if you live in a sun-deprived country like me). Natural light regulates your sleep–wake cycle and promotes the release of the sleep hormones needed to help you to hit the hay.

Tip 7: Siesta. A well-timed power nap is an absolute gamechanger. I have just spent a few days in Seville doing as the locals do, snoozing for 20 minutes every day in the afternoon, and I felt glorious. My feelings are corroborated by numerous studies that show that a short 20-minute nap can boost alertness, enhance creativity and improve cognitive performance. I am going to do this more when at home.

In the wise words of Matthew Walker, 'Sleep is your superpower'. Embrace it, cherish it and let it transform your life.
Sweet dreams.

34
HAPPINESS VS JOY

Do you know the difference between joy and happiness? Hats off to you if you do, because I certainly did not before researching and writing this chapter. The clearest and most succinct distinction that I have found between the two is that happiness is typically achieved externally, while joy is something we cultivate and find within ourselves.

Time to take a closer look. We feel happy when something external happens to us, such as receiving a gift, getting a pay rise or receiving a compliment after smashing the pitch with a potential client. These experiences bring us a sense of pleasure and gratification, but they are often fleeting and do not necessarily lead to a long-lasting feeling of happiness.

On the other hand, joy is a much deeper feeling that persists no matter and often despite the circumstances. Joy can be often born of suffering, and it comes when we can make peace with who we are, what we have and what we think we lack. It is not something we can buy or acquire; it comes from within. 'I am a good man and I try my best, that is all I can do.' I do not think I would feel a third of the joy I feel on a daily basis if it were not for what I have been through. I think back and it hurts every time, but I am immensely grateful. I would not be writing this for you now if my life had panned out differently.

It is so easy to fall into the trap of seeking external sources of happiness when we have had a rubbish day at work, or even when we are having a good one. We might reach for a piece of chocolate, a glass of wine, *insert guilty pleasure here*. These hedonic pleasures offer a temporary reprieve from our problems, but they are fleeting and often leave us feeling guilty or unsatisfied and we reach for a second, third, fourth, each one less satisfying than the first.

This is where eudaimonia comes in. Eudaimonia (hedonia's self-righteous cousin) in its most simple form is the feeling (most typically explained as joy) that comes from living with a sense of meaning, living with purpose and striving to reach our potential. It is the deeper joy that comes from within, rather than external sources.

Nietzsche once said, 'He who has a why can deal with any how.' By finding meaning and purpose in our lives, we can experience a deeper sense of joy that is not dependent on external circumstances. The best and equally harrowing example of this for me is Viktor Frankl. For four years of his life he was imprisoned in a concentration camp, surviving on the most meagre rations you could possibly imagine and not knowing whether he was going to live to see the next day.

His experience of surviving those four years became a global symbol of human resilience and determination. He believed that the primary force that motivates people in life is to find meaning, which he called the 'will to meaning' (his eudaimonia). His will to meaning was to publish his memoirs, which he memorized word for word and wrote upon his release. How he managed this is beyond me, I struggle to remember where I put my keys at the best of times, let alone write and remember an entire book in a concentration camp.

Frankl observed that those who found meaning in their experience of the concentration camps were the ones who survived the Holocaust:

> The death rate in the week between Christmas 1944 and New
> Year 1945 increased in camp beyond all previous experience.
> In his opinion, the explanation for this increase did not lie
> in the harder working conditions or the deterioration of our
> food supplies or a change of weather or new epidemics. It was
> simply that the majority of the prisoners had lived in the naive
> hope that they would be home again by Christmas. As the time
> drew near and there was no encouraging news, the prisoners
> lost courage and disappointment overcame them...[90]

Frankl's insights have helped many people around the world who face existential questions, giving them direction and purpose in their lives. To find a purpose and a why in life can be priceless, as it can help individuals overcome any challenge that life throws at them. Frankl's ideas on the will to meaning offer a powerful message of hope and inspiration, reminding us that even in the face of adversity, we can find meaning and purpose that will guide us through life and sustain us much better than a second bottle of Sauvignon Blanc, as good as it is.

A friend actually bought me Viktor Frankl's *Man's Search for Meaning* at a time when I was really struggling. I was so anxious that every time I left my front door I felt like I was going to wet myself and was wearing an adult diaper at the time that he gave me this book (this is just how my anxiety used to show up). My experience does not compare to Frankl's, nor am I suggesting it does. His teachings helped me understand that what I had been through and what I will go through will be the fuel I need to help others, hence the writing of this book and what I do every single day.

I believe that pursuing happiness and indulging in some hedonic pleasure is something we should all still do – I am certainly not an aesthetic hermit or suggesting otherwise – but choosing joy is something we should make space for and prioritize every single day. The absolute best time of day for me was 12.15 pm, when I would step away from my desk and give my nan a call. It is something that started in the pandemic and that I loved every day since. It was the best time of day, every day. She passed away unexpectedly on 24 April 2023, while I was writing this book, and I will never get the chance to call her again. Joy is something we make space for every single day. I am devastated she is no longer here, but I am hugely grateful for making the time every day and have zero regrets.

So how can we cultivate a sense of eudaimonia and a feeling of joy in our lives, not just for ourselves, but for others too? Oh, and don't worry, you don't have to give up the ice cream.

Steger et al's 2008 *Being Good by Doing Good* study[91] assessed whether eudaimonic behaviour resulted in a better sense of wellbeing. The team found that eudaimonic behaviours had consistently stronger relations to positive wellbeing – daily meaning in life and life satisfaction – than pleasure or material goods, aka hedonic behaviours. These are the following eudaimonic behaviours they used for their study, which will be our tips for this chapter:

Tip 1: Volunteering one's time.

Tip 2: Giving money to someone in need.

Tip 3: Writing out one's future goals.

Tip 4: Expressing gratitude for another's actions, either written or verbal.

Tip 5: Carefully listening to another's point of view.

Tip 6: Confiding in someone about something that is of personal importance.

Tip 7: Persevering at valued goals in spite of obstacles.

We are going to hand over to the one and only Viktor Frankl to finish this chapter off for us:

> Don't aim at success. The more you aim at it and make it a target, the more you are going to miss it. For success, like happiness, cannot be pursued; it must ensue, and it only does so as the unintended side effect of one's personal dedication to a cause greater.

Imagine this scenario: it's 3 pm, you're on a diet, and you have just finished your seventh consecutive video call. Someone offers you a slice of millionaire's shortbread, and you think, 'Oh, one won't hurt'. At this point, it would be easier to solve nuclear fission than to resist that delicious treat. Sound familiar? Feel free to remove 'slice of millionaire's shortbread' and insert another guilty pleasure.

That is because willpower, like any other muscle, fatigues as it is used again and again throughout the day. It's not something you have or lack, but rather something that rises and falls. Many people experience this feeling, which is also known as ego depletion. The theory behind ego depletion is that willpower is connected to a limited reserve of mental energy. Once you have used up that energy, you are more likely to lose self-control. And the best know this and take steps to configure their day and decisions to work in their favour.

How many decisions do you make every day?

According to various sources, we make around 35,000 decisions every day.[92] That is an astounding number and a recipe for decision fatigue. As we make more and more decisions throughout the day, our willpower decreases, and we become more susceptible to temptation. Researchers at Ben Gurion University in Israel and Columbia University examined more than 1,000 decisions by eight Israeli judges who ruled on convicts' parole requests. Judges granted 65 per cent of requests they heard at the beginning of the day's session and almost none at the end. Right after a snack break, approvals jumped back to 65 per cent again.[93] This is called the hungry judge effect. Another study found that 62 per cent of instore purchases were made impulsively[94] – you know the old saying, 'Never go shopping hungry'. Always a bad idea. The list goes on and on and the studies all indicate that willpower is finite.

However, recent research suggests that we might have been thinking about willpower all wrong. The theory of ego depletion might not be true, and holding onto this idea could be detrimental to our happiness and success. A study published in *The Proceedings of the National Academy of Sciences* found that people who believed their willpower had been exhausted after an arduous task were re-energized by sugary lemonade, whereas those who did not believe that their willpower was a finite resource and expendable had no reaction.[95] This suggests that ego depletion might be caused by self-defeating thoughts rather than any biological limitation.

Other studies have also found that believing we are powerless to resist something can make us more likely to give in. For example, studies of cigarette smokers found that those who believed they were powerless to resist were most likely to fall off the wagon after they quit.[96] This theory could be applied to other things as well, such as working out, dieting or anything really.

According to Michael Inzlicht, a psychology professor at the University of Toronto, willpower is not a finite resource but behaves more like an emotion.[97] Similar to emotions like sadness or excitement, willpower fluctuates based on our environment, circumstances and emotional state. This understanding of willpower has significant implications for how we direct our attention and efforts. If mental energy is more like an emotion than a fuel tank, it can be managed and utilized accordingly. For instance, when we face a difficult task, it is more productive and healthy to view a lack of motivation as temporary rather than believing that we are exhausted, the battery is empty and we need to stop.

However, there are times when a lack of motivation is not temporary. Our feelings provide valuable information that our conscious mind might overlook. If a lack of mental energy or willpower persists, we should pay attention to the feeling, treating it like we would our emotions. Willpower can serve as a useful tool to guide our decision making and help us identify tasks that are worth our time and effort. By working alongside our logical capabilities, willpower can help us discover new paths that do not require us to engage in activities we fundamentally do not want to do.

The way we speak to ourselves is crucial. Believing that we lack self-control can become a self-fulfilling prophecy. Instead of blaming ourselves for our failures, we should show self-compassion by speaking kindly to ourselves when we face setbacks. This approach can help shift our mindset and allow us to use our willpower as a tool to achieve our goals.

Whether or not you think willpower is finite, an emotion or anything else, the following tips might help you to bolster yours:

Tip 1: Plan your daily decisions the night before. Think Mark Zuckerberg and his T-shirts, or Steve Jobs and his black turtlenecks. By reducing the number of decisions you need to make each day, you conserve your willpower for the important things.

Tip 2: Do the most important thing first. Whether willpower is expendable or not, we often feel most motivated first thing in the morning, so use that time to tackle your biggest challenges.

Tip 3: Commit and plan. Do not just say, 'If I have time, I will go to the gym.' Instead, plan to train at 7.30 am before work. The former will never happen, so don't kid yourself.

Tip 4: Social pressure. Yes, I do like this one. Share your commitment with friends and family for some social pressure. I do this all the time, from book writing to ultra marathons. Having someone to hold you accountable can be a powerful motivator.

Tip 5: Snack time. If you do have to make a decision later, have a snack. Eating something sweet or drinking something sugary can help replenish your energy that you are lacking right now. It is not a long-term solution, but it can help you get through a tough moment. As we discussed, this may not help willpower at all, but it is a great excuse for a treat regardless! Not that you need an excuse for a slice of cake.

Tip 6: Avoid the scenario. Trying to stop drinking? Don't go to the pub. Willpower, however you look at it, can be tested easily and does not always pass the test. If you do not put it to the test it cannot fail. Consider your environment and whether it is setting you up to succeed or fail.

Whether you are a judge, a shopper, quitting smoking or something different entirely, remember – your willpower like your emotions will fluctuate, so use it on what really matters to you. Oh, and grab something sweet. Because, well, why not?

YOUR EMAILS ARE KILLING YOU

If sitting down is the new smoking, then emails are the new sitting down; our emails are slowly choking the life out of us and we do not even realize it. It was your manager, in the office, with the ton of emails who did it, not Colonel Mustard with the steel pipe in the kitchen. Have you ever spent hours on email and felt like you were wound tight, anxious and unable to relax? Do you find that even when you stop working, your mind keeps racing, unable to settle down? OK, let me flip that around: have you ever spent time in your inbox and felt energized? I think I know the answer. Most of us are actually suffering from what psychologist Linda Stone calls 'email apnea'.[98]

Email apnea is characterized by shallow breathing or breath-holding while doing email or sitting in front of a screen. According to Stone, it affects more than 80 per cent of us. Interestingly, as I was writing this sentence, I thought about my breath and realized I was not breathing; I think it is more about screens than emails, but that is just my opinion. Email apnea happens because we unconsciously slump and hold our breath while working, becoming so engrossed in whatever we are doing that we forget to breathe properly. That is just a crazy sentence is it not? You have been breathing since you were born and email makes us forget. This can cause a cacophony of mental, emotional and physical problems, from increased stress levels and musculoskeletal issues to fatigue and a decreased ability to focus.

Don't believe me? Spend 10 minutes on emails and you will be reminded of the above.

As we discussed in Chapter 5, 'And breathe', the average adult in the UK spends over seven hours per day in front of a screen. That's a lot of lost breaths! And with the pandemic forcing many of us to work from home and rely even more heavily on screen time, the problem is only getting worse. But do not despair, my oxygen-deprived friends, there are simple steps you can take to reduce the impact of email on your health:

Tip 1: Breathe. Starting with a glaringly obvious one, it is important to keep on breathing. Nice. Focus on the inhale and exhale in your abdomen for 10 seconds, in and out. This simple exercise can help to counteract the shallow breathing caused by email apnea, promoting deeper, more relaxed breathing patterns.

Tip 2: Regular breaks. Set a timer to remind yourself to step away every 25 minutes or so, or use an auto-scheduling tool to remind you to take breaks throughout the day. You might take a quick walk around the block, do some stretches or simply stand up and stretch your arms and legs. Whatever you choose to do, the key is to take time away from the screen and let your mind and body relax.

Tip 3: Shut eye. Shut your eyes for a few seconds or look off into the distance with a soft gaze. Giving your eyes a break can help to reduce eye strain and fatigue, as well as help you to refocus your attention when you return to your work.

By taking these simple steps, we can wrestle our breath back from those pesky emails.

But the problem does not end with email apnea. Oh, joy. Email can also be a major source of stress and overwhelm in our lives and it certainly is not helping us be more productive, so why do we do it? According to a survey from Adobe, the average employee spends 3.1 hours per day checking and responding to work emails, with many workers checking their inbox outside of work hours as well.[99] Oh, and another 2.5 hours on personal email. This constant email checking can lead to a sense of always being 'on', never able to fully disconnect from work and recharge. People even check personal email while watching TV (60 per cent), using the bathroom (40 per cent), talking on the phone (35 per cent), working out (16 per cent) and even driving (14 per cent).

To combat email overload, it is not only important, but crucial to set boundaries around when and how you check your email:

Bonus tip 1: Timebox. Try designating specific times of day to check and respond to messages, rather than constantly checking throughout the day, e.g. three windows: 8.45–9.15, 12.00–12.30 and 17.00–17.30.

Bonus tip 2: Configuration. Utilize tools like email filters or priority labels to help you manage your inbox more effectively, prioritizing the most important messages and letting the rest wait until you have more time, or never.

Bonus tip 3: Unsubscribe. Some of my friends have inboxes with 10,000+ unread emails and that makes me feel slightly nauseous. Every time I receive a newsletter or something I am not interested in I automatically unsubscribe – personal or work. My traffic has been dramatically reduced and so has the anxiety that comes with it.

Bonus tip 4: Silence. Turn off all email notifications: no banners, no noises, no nothing. Check it when it suits you.

Bonus tip 5: Did that have to be an email? Instead of using email as your default mode of communication, consider whether an instant message, phone call or face-to-face conversation might be more appropriate. Sometimes, a quick chat can be more efficient and effective than a long email chain, reducing the stress and time demands of email communication. Others may begin to follow your lead. We can hope anyway.

Remember, an email is basically someone else's to-do list. Check it when it suits you and respond at a time that suits you. Just because the message is instantaneous, does not mean your response has to be.

YOU VS A GOLDFISH – ATTENTION

We juggle numerous tasks simultaneously, believing that it is the most efficient way to get things done. You are probably holding this book in one hand while cooking a spaghetti Bolognese with the other and rocking the baby with your foot. The vast majority of the time you are not multitasking but single tasking, and badly – people who think they can multitask are often the worst. Somewhat unsurprisingly, multitasking can actually be detrimental to our productivity and focus. As we switch our attention between tasks, this leads to errors, longer completion times and decreased performance. Constant multitasking can and does also lead to stress, anxiety and burnout in the worst of cases.[100] How happy are you when you are jumping between 17 competing priorities? Overjoyed, right?

Multitasking often goes by another name nowadays and that is context switching. 'What is in a name? That which we call a rose, by any other name would smell just as sweet.' Thank you, Romeo. Whatever you call it, it comes with a high cost, a very high cost – an estimated annual cost of $450 billion globally.[101] This in no small part owes to the fact that context switching has been found to result in a 40 per cent loss in productivity.[102] Delightful.

Dr Gloria Mark of the University of California found out that it takes an average of 23 minutes and 15 seconds to fully recover from a distraction and return to a task.[103] The study also found that, on average, workers switch tasks every three minutes. Therefore, according to Dr Mark's work, it would seem that we are never able to focus and we find ourselves in a constant state of heightened anxiety and alertness, just waiting for the next digital request. Oh, and don't forget to breathe (like we discussed in the previous chapter).

It's time to say hasta la vista to multitasking (in an American-Austrian accent), to say au revoir to context switching, to say tschüss to distraction. But you don't have time to do that, do you? You're far too busy.

When we are distraction free, though, during peak periods of attention, we are able to focus for 1.5–2 hours. But how do we know when to schedule this focus time? We don't have all day, do we?

1 Stop and evaluate your attention multiple times throughout the day.

2 At each evaluation, record the time and answer these two questions on a scale of 1–5 (higher scores indicate higher periods of attention):
   – How absorbed are you in your current task?
   – How challenged are you with your current task?

3 Do this for three to five days and review the data for patterns.

4 Using the data, identify your peak attention windows and plan your most essential work during this time.

Focus time for me is about 10 am, once the morning emails/planning are done and before the inevitable slump after lunch. When is yours? Work it out, block it out in your calendar and protect that time like your life depends on it.

Sometimes it feels like we are fighting a losing battle, but there are things that we can do to fight distraction and maintain our attention:

Tip 1: Unfocus time. We are not able to be at full attention all of the time; just like we require rest between sets when lifting weights, our attention spans require rest.

Tip 2: Recharge. When our attention begins to fade, it's time to embrace simple tasks like taking a walk, washing the dishes, making a coffee or even tidying up to give your mind a break and rejuvenate your ability to focus.

Tip 3: Distraction free. When it's time to focus, it's time to eliminate distractions. Time to silence notifications, close your email, put instrumental music on (it helps me anyway – check out Chapter 51, 'Music is the answer') and leave your phone in the other room.

Tip 4: Your own worst enemy. You will interrupt yourself, it is just a matter of when. Keep an eye out for your self-interruption triggers. Just one peak at TikTok won't hurt... two hours later. When tempted to self-interrupt, stop and ask yourself, 'Do I really need to do this right now?' Probably not.

Sorry, what were you saying?

38

THE 80/20 RULE

Have you ever heard of the 80/20 rule? It's also known as the Pareto principle and it suggests that 20 per cent of our efforts yield 80 per cent of the results. At first you think, that can't be true. Mr Vilfredo de Pareto developed the principle over a century ago, but it is still discussed, debated and utilized today. Now you are thinking, 'You had my curiosity but now you have my attention, Mr Hopkins.' (That was Leonardo Di Caprio in *Django Unchained* if you didn't know already – what a film!)

Now, just imagine that by harnessing the power of Vilfredo de Pareto you could achieve a significant portion of your wellbeing-based goals and aspirations by focusing on a small fraction of your actions or habits. Time to maximize the bang for our buck regarding our time and effort.

Time to turn our attention to our everyday behaviours and habits. Did you know that roughly 45 per cent of our daily behaviours are driven by habits? They are automatic and often done in exactly the same place, according to a study from the University of Southern California.[104] That's a substantial chunk of our lives being carried out on autopilot. One more thing – not all habits are created equal. Some have a more significant impact than others.

In 2022, I walked 860 km across Spain in 19 days (the Camino De Santiago – the French Way), doing 19 consecutive ultra marathons self-supported – that's a story for another day. After I finished my pilgrimage and arrived home, I really struggled to get back into my routine. My sleeping pattern shifted by just one or two hours, and it threw my whole day off balance. The alarm would go off at 6 am, but instead of jumping out of bed and heading for the coffee machine, I was reaching around to switch off my alarm clock and re-roll into a human burrito: 'not today, world'. No morning work-out, no meditation and definitely no cold shower. It was a domino effect that left me feeling completely off track. I never got around to it after work, either.

But I did a bit of digging and here's what I found I needed to do: focus on my cornerstone habit, which is also known as a keystone habit.[105] This one habit sets the tone for the rest of my day; it's the one habit upon which the others rest. For me, it's going to bed at 9.30 pm. When I go to bed at this time and read for as long as my eyes let me (retiring my phone at least 30 minutes beforehand – see Chapter 33 on the power of sleep for more), I'm able to get up as my alarm goes off, swinging my legs out of bed and grabbing that coffee – often making it with one eye open. Once I accomplish that, everything else seems to fall into place. The morning workout happens, meditation brings a moment of peace and the cold shower invigorates me. It is quite amazing how one small thing can make everything else easier.

So, what about you? What are your cornerstone habits? Have you ever thought about the habits that create a positive ripple effect? They could be the missing key to unlocking Pandora's box, which contains a more productive, fulfilling and balanced existence. It really doesn't have to be anything complex either. Perhaps it's simply that morning cup of coffee that sparks creativity, a daily walk that clears your mind or a few minutes of journalling that brings clarity to your thoughts. Identify your cornerstone habits and make them non-negotiable, creating space for them every single day. Trust me, they can and do make a world of difference.

Now, let us circle back to the Pareto principle. If 20 per cent of our efforts generate 80 per cent of our value at work, imagine how it applies to our wellbeing. Just 20 per cent of the things we do for our overall wellbeing can provide a significantly larger return on investment. For me, it's 45 minutes of circuit training. This simple workout not only improves my physical fitness, but also boosts my mental and emotional wellbeing. It is a trifecta of sweaty deliciousness in a short amount of time.

With cornerstones and 80/20s in mind, take a moment to reflect on your own wellbeing. What does that 20 per cent look like for you? Is it a workout, spending quality time with loved ones or dedicating moments to self-care, whatever that looks like for you? Remember that what works for one does not work for another, so beware any advice givers – me included. Identify those key activities and habits that bring you the most value and make them a priority.

My cornerstone habit is going to bed at 9.30. This enables me to make time for and prioritize my 20 per cent habit, which is circuit training. Your cornerstone can also be part of your 20 per cent, they do not have to be separate.

Here are some practical tips to help you make the most of the 80/20 rule and identify your cornerstone habits:

Tip 1: Identify your cornerstone habits. Take some time to reflect on your daily routines and habits. Which actions have the most significant impact on your overall wellbeing and productivity? These are your cornerstone habits. As we discussed, they do not need to be complex, often the opposite. It could be something as simple as a morning exercise routine, setting aside time for focused work or practising mindfulness. Once you identify these habits, make them non-negotiable and prioritize them every day – see Chapter 11, 'Non-negotiable wellbeing', for more on this.

Tip 2: Streamline the schedule. Apply the 80/20 rule to your schedule by identifying the most important tasks or activities that generate the greatest wellbeing return on investment. Focus on completing those tasks first before moving on to less impactful ones. By streamlining your schedule and focusing on the priorities, you will free up more time and energy for what truly matters. Conversely, by focusing on the most important things that energize you, you will find you will have the energy and focus to be able to do everything else. If you want to, you are also entitled to just chill out. You have earned it.

Tip 3: Re-assess, re-evaluate and re-adjust. Sit down now and again and think about how your cornerstone habits and the 20 per cent activities are impacting your life. Are they still providing the desired benefits? Are there any new habits or actions that could yield greater returns? Stay flexible and open to adjustments as your priorities and circumstances evolve. This is meant to happen; it means you are growing and developing. Regular evaluation allows you to fine-tune your habits and ensure you are focusing on what has the most positive outsized impact on your wellbeing.

Life is short, you're busy and have a lot on, therefore you need to optimize your wellbeing efforts. We just need to focus on the vital few habits and actions that create the largest positive wellbeing ripples and provide the greatest returns. So, it's time to embrace the power of our cornerstone habits and the 20 per cent that truly matters.

Imagine waking up every morning with £1,440 in your pocket. Sweet. You would immediately ask, what's the catch? The catch is that you have to spend it all by midnight; otherwise, whatever is left will vanish. You would be intentional and make sure you spent, invested and saved every penny, right? Sadly, I am not going to give you £1,440 every morning – apologies. However, you are credited with 1,440 minutes every day and, just like those imaginary pounds, they slip away if not used wisely. So, how often do you ask yourself, 'How am I going to spend my time today?'

We live in a world where it feels like we have a million and one things to do but never enough hours in the day. Time management is not only a nice to have but a crucial skill and not just one you lie about on your CV as well as 'Excel skills'.

When you consider productivity, what do you think about? Is it about an individual who is very busy, but getting it done, or do you consider someone who has time, who is careful with what they say yes to, someone who ruthlessly prioritizes the things they need to do daily to be their best self? Productivity is not about doing everything efficiently, effectively, economically and being a 'machine'. Rather it is about choosing what not to do and saying no. It's about making conscious decisions about where to invest your minutes. If you do not respect your time, no one else is going to. You could be the most effective and productive employee on your team, but if you say yes to everything, your effectiveness will begin to diminish, as will your wellbeing.

I wish I could say yes to every request for 'just five minutes of your time', but if I did, I wouldn't even have time to brush my teeth before going to bed. It's essential to think twice before committing to anything and avoid impulsive responses. Your time, energy and resources are being sequestered, so respond slowly and deliberately.

Introducing the slow yes, which challenges our tendency to say 'yes' as our initial response to just about any offer. Especially in the UK, it hurts us so much to say no, so instead we say, 'Not really, I'm good, I don't think so, I would love to but…' I have ended up at numerous parties, events, meetings and thought to myself, 'What the hell am I doing here? Why did I say yes to this?'

Contrary to popular belief, wellbeing is not about adding more to our already overflowing plates. It is often not about more, but about less. It is about being selective and knowing when to say no to. If your answer to a request is not a definite yes, then it should be no. No feeling guilty for protecting your time and energy. When pressured to make quick decisions, make 'no' your default answer. Only say 'yes' after carefully analysing the situation and ensuring it aligns with your goals and values. This helps me: tell yourself, if you would not do it tomorrow, it doesn't matter that it is in five months, it's still a no.

The slow yes urges us to be more intentional in our choices and commitments, allowing us to create and protect space for the things in our lives that matter and – this is a crazy notion – some time to relax. I know, I know, the thought makes you uncomfortable, but give it a go some time. By learning to politely decline invitations and prioritize our time, we can find some semblance of balance between personal and professional life. Few things are genuinely a priority and it is up to us to make those choices.

Warren Buffet spends 80 per cent of his day reading. He likes to be informed before he makes a business-changing decision. He once said this about defending his time: 'The difference between successful people and very successful people is that very successful people say "no" to almost everything.'[106]

But how are you to know what to say no to? If only there were a super helpful and easy tool to help you with this. Introducing the Eisenhower Decision Matrix, an incredibly simple yet powerful tool to help you prioritize effectively. Learn to distinguish between what is urgent and what is important.

Dwight D Eisenhower was a president of the United States and Supreme Commander of the Allied Expeditionary Force in Europe during WWII, so we can assume he was a pretty busy man. He once noted that 'when our affairs seem to be in crisis, we are almost compelled to give our first attention to the urgent present rather than to the important future'. To resolve this issue, he created the Eisenhower Matrix. Let's get into it:

Tip 1: The Eisenhower Matrix. Picture a 2x2 matrix where you place tasks accordingly:

- Important and Urgent: These are the tasks that demand your immediate attention. Handle them promptly and efficiently.

- Important and Not Urgent: These tasks are significant but don't require immediate action. Schedule them for later to ensure they receive the attention they deserve.

- Not Important and Urgent: These tasks might seem urgent, but they don't contribute significantly to your goals or wellbeing. Delegate them to others whenever possible.

- Not Important and Not Urgent: These tasks are time-wasters. Eliminate them from your to-do list to free up valuable time for what truly matters.

By using the Eisenhower Decision Matrix, you can prioritize, delegate and eliminate tasks according to their importance and urgency. It is a practical way to make the most of your limited time and prioritize what you need each day to be your best self!

Tip 2: 5 × nos. Challenge yourself to say 'no' five times this week. No 'maybes', 'I would love to but…', 'I will check', etc; instead, a polite 'no, thank you'. This is not just of benefit to yourself, but to the organizer of the event who can plan accordingly and will not order food and drink only for you to bail at the last minute. Which is so annoying.

Just as you would not give your wallet or purse to anyone who asked for it, consider your time just as valuable, if not more so. Utilize the Eisenhower Decision Matrix to prioritize effectively and make conscious choices, embracing the slow yes and quick no. To quote a Tweet from author Les Brown: 'In every day, there are 1,440 minutes. That means we have 1,440 daily opportunities to make a positive impact.' So let's not waste them.

If I offered you £5 million today or a magic penny that doubles in value every day for 31 days, which would you choose? It's tempting to take the £5 million, right? But let's look at what happens when you pick the sweet £5 million and leave me with the solitary old penny.

By day 10, you would have a cool £5 million in your bank account, providing you had not gone on a spending spree, while I would be sitting pretty with a modest £5.12. That's barely enough to buy a half pint in central London. Fast forward to day 20, and I would have £5,243, which is still a whopping £4,994,757 less than you. Ok, please don't look so smug – you can smell there is a twist here, right?

Now, let us jump to day 29. I would have £2.7 million, just £2.3 million behind you. Suddenly, you are starting to question your decision. But it's only on day 30 that things really take a turn. I would have £5.3 million, and when the smoke settles on day 31, the damage is clear, and you are deeply regretting your choice as I triumphantly count my £10,737,418.24.

So, what is the lesson here? Small smart choices with consistency over time equal a radical difference. And this formula does not just apply to finances; it works for your best self bank account too; small, smart wellbeing choices with consistency over time equal a radical difference. Focus on making positive deposits, reducing the withdrawals, and watch that best self bank account balance rise. Oh, and by the way, if anyone happens to know where I can get my hands on a magic penny, slide into my DMs, please.

Now, let me tell you what I consider to be one of the most mind-blowing stories I have ever heard. Can you imagine writing a book? (The fact I have written one still blows my mind.) Not just any book, but one written solely with your left eyelid? Sounds crazy, right? Well, Jean-Dominique Bauby, former editor-in-chief of *Elle*, completed the unimaginable and incomprehensible feat. After suffering a stroke in his sleep one day, he woke up with locked-in syndrome and could only communicate by moving his left eyelid.

But Bauby was not ready to give up, far from it. He wrote a book called *The Diving Bell and the Butterfly* about his experience of being trapped inside his own body. And here is the real crazy bit, it took him over 200,000 blinks to complete it. Each word took him over two minutes to communicate, totalling an estimated 78,936 minutes, 1,315.6 hours, 54.81 days. Absolutely incredible. It just goes to show that incredible things happen when we keep showing up. One blink at a time. Sure, intensity may fluctuate, but consistency is the key.

Now, time to apply the compound effect to weight loss. No need to worry, I will not be recommending keto, Atkins, carnivore or needing to strictly eat animal organs and even their dangly bits – remember that guy? Nope. How would you like to shed 20 pounds this year without going on a diet or even stepping foot in the gym? Well, here is a juicy little trick for you. If you bounce your leg the entire time you are at work, for eight hours/480 minutes per day, you will burn approximately 300 calories (173) – of course, depending on your body size it may be more or less. To put this in perspective, a cheeseburger from McDonald's has about 290 calories. So, you can take a break for 16 minutes and smash down a cheeseburger guilt-free.

This could be the first wellbeing book advocating the consumption of McDonald's cheeseburgers. I can't wait for that sponsorship deal! Wellbeing is not so much about big actions, fancy technology applications or complex solutions; it is actually about making a series of small, smart choices consistently over time. Every little bit adds up and over time the impact has the potential to be massive. The most important thing is that you do something. Can't make it to the gym? No need to worry about it, just shake a leg.

When I started my social media wellbeing journey over three years ago, I would spend hours writing, recording, uploading and would receive one or two likes. I did not let it deter me, as I know Rome was not built in a day. I have since posted over 1,500 times and am now engaging between 100,000 and 250,000 people per week, which is more people than the entirety of my hometown Hastings (98,000). It took a year and a half to reach a million people and now I am doing that every month. Magical stuff happens when you continue to turn up.

If you post once per week, you are in the top 1 per cent of LinkedIn users. You might get one or two likes at first, but you never know who you are helping. Helping one person might not change the world, but it might change the world for that one person. The best way to learn is by doing. Yes, it's scary at first, but trust me, in three years you will be very proud of yourself and grateful that you got started. Check out Chapter 26, 'What are you waiting for?' for more on this.

You get the message: little and often is key. No matter what you are doing.

Regardless, it can be difficult if not impossible sometimes to stay motivated as improvements are rarely visible in the short term; however, it does not mean they are not happening. You know what it's like when you are trying to lose weight, stepping on a scale every day and expecting to see the number change drastically. That's not how it works, but you know that already. Lasting wins require a lifestyle change rather than short-term bursts of energy and effort. The progress we want to see arises as a lagging indicator of consistent effort and dedication.

Ryan Holiday wrote 'All success is a lagging indicator.'[107] He explains that when things go well, whether it is a productive writing day or hitting a personal record at the gym, it is the result of the hours and hours spent researching, practising and preparing behind the scenes. Think about it. Hitting a personal record on the bench press is a lagging indicator of the discipline and hard work you put into your workouts. Receiving a promotion is a lagging indicator of the quality work you have consistently delivered. Delivering a keynote speech with confidence is a lagging indicator of the extensive preparation you invested in it.

So, remember that although you may not see success in the short term, we know that the little and often approach will yield the success we are looking for – the success may just be lagging a bit. We cannot expect immediate results or instant transformations; we should instead put our energy into showing up consistently, making those small choices that align with our goals and giving them time to compound and create a lasting impact. Whether it is saving money, pursuing your passion, improving your health or enhancing your relationships, the key lies in the daily actions you take. Stay committed, stay consistent and trust in the power of those small steps. Tip time:

Tip 1: Little bites. How do you eat an elephant? One bite at a time. Break down your goals into smaller tasks or habits that you can incorporate into your daily routine – and I am talking really small. Want to walk more? Just make a promise to put your shoes on and step outside. If you don't feel like it when you are laced up, no problem, come back inside. We are building the habit for now and chances are that when your shoes are on you will go for a walk.

Tip 2: Same time same place. Establish a specific time or routine dedicated to whatever it is you want to do. It could be as simple as setting aside 15 minutes each morning for meditation, writing or exercise. Consistency is key, so make it a non-negotiable part of your day. I like to meditate after working out in the morning and for some strange reason I like to do it in the shower.

Tip 3: Celebrate the little wins. Recognize and celebrate the progress you make along the way, no matter how small. Each small step forward is a victory which reinforces your commitment to the process and deserves to be celebrated. Reward yourself for your efforts, whether it is treating yourself to something you enjoy or sharing your achievements with others.

Tip 4: Build accountability. Find an accountability partner or join a community of like-minded individuals who share similar wellbeing aspirations. You can also track your progress using apps, journals or habit trackers to hold yourself accountable. I have repeated this a few times, but it works. If you treasure it, measure it.

Tip 5: Patience is key. As we have discussed, lasting change takes time. It is very easy to get discouraged when we do not see immediate results, but trust in the power of consistency and the compounding effect of your efforts over time. Stay committed, stay patient and trust that your consistent actions will yield significant results.

The journey of a thousand miles begins with a single step and it is the accumulation of those small steps that leads to remarkable transformations. Now, if you will excuse me, I'm off to get a cheeseburger and look for that penny.

41
RAIN OR LIQUID SUNSHINE?

If I were to offer you a million pounds this morning, would you take it?

Of course you would. How could anyone resist such a tantalizing offer? You would be floating on cloud nine, would you not? I reckon all of your problems and negative emotions would just magically vanish into thin air. Mine certainly would. No one would be able to irritate me, annoy me or ruin that day, right? Not even Lucy from Marketing *shakes fist*.

But what if I added a spicy little twist? You can have the million pounds – or better yet, make it a billion. However, if you take it you will not wake up tomorrow. Suddenly, the offer loses its appeal. The truth is, the simple act of waking up today is worth more than all the money in the world. Now, I know this may sound like some motivational mumbo jumbo, but bear with me. It is simply about appreciating the value of each day. It is about realizing that the very act of being alive is a precious gift.

The mere chance of you being born is 1 in 400 trillion.[108] Yep, you read that right. But what does a number like that even look like? A Buddhist proverb paints the picture: Imagine that there is a lifebuoy thrown somewhere in an ocean and there is only one turtle in all the oceans, swimming underwater somewhere. The probability that you will appear and exist is as small as the probability that that turtle will stick its head out of the water in the middle of this life-buoy, in a single attempt. This makes me feel rather lucky and puts a little spring in my step when I think about the sheer lunacy of it – and I hope it does the same for you.

I have a little scenario for you. It begins to rain in Montego Bay, Jamaica – is it rain or is it liquid sunshine? Well, that depends on whether you ask the British tourist or the Jamaican fisherman. It's certainly true that life can throw unfair, upsetting or dangerous situations our way and in those cases it is important to attempt to find a solution or walk away as fast as our legs will take us. However, not everything that happens needs to be immediately linked to our internal narrative and whether it is 'good' or 'bad' – see Chapter 24, 'In my humble opinion', for more.

We are the architects of our reality and we have the power to shape our own perceptions. So, let us take hold of the pen and draw a better picture for ourselves – drawing skills not required. The sooner we realize that we can make our own luck and write our own story, the sooner we gain a tremendous amount of power and that power remains ours as long as we refuse to hand it over to something or someone else.

I know what you are thinking at this point: 'That's all well and good, Ryan, but these are just stories and you don't know me. I'm not a Jamaican fisherman, I am unlucky, life doesn't work out like that for me.' A lot of people feel this way, you're not alone. This is the reason Richard Wiseman, a psychologist from the University of Hertfordshire, dedicated 10 years to the Luck Project, exploring how luck plays a role in our lives. He wanted to understand how chance opportunities come about and their impact on our lives, examining the difference between self-professed lucky and unlucky people.

The study revealed that luck is not a magical force that belongs to only the rich and powerful, but is simply influenced and often determined by our thoughts, behaviours and perceptions.[109] No one is born lucky or unlucky, despite what most of us think. The self-confessed 'lucky' people generate their own good fortune via four basic principles: they are skilled at creating and noticing chance opportunities, making lucky decisions by listening to their intuition, creating self-fulfilling prophecies via positive expectations and adopting a resilient attitude that transforms bad luck into good. 'Unlucky' people, on the other hand, tend to do the opposite and often miss chance opportunities due to their tense, worried and fixed mindset.

To see if the so-called 'unlucky' people could turn their luck around, Wiseman enrolled his participants in 'luck school', where he put them through a series of exercises to increase their luck. The results were pretty amazing. After one month of enrollment, 80 per cent of people reported themselves as happier, more satisfied with their lives and, most importantly, luckier. The lucky ones became luckier, and the unlucky turned lucky.

Here's how:

Tip 1: Embrace new possibilities. Instead of fixating on a single goal, maintain an open mind and observe your surroundings. By cultivating an open attitude and exploring fresh opportunities, you enhance your chances of stumbling upon fortunate circumstances.

Tip 2: Focus on the bright side. Dedicating all your attention to negativity can dampen your enthusiasm and hinder future prospects. Shifting your perspective from complaining about minor setbacks to appreciating the absence of worse outcomes makes it easier to venture into uncharted territory.

Tip 3: Break free from the ordinary. Falling into repetitive patterns, whether in social interactions, eating habits or work routines, can lead to monotony. By stepping outside your comfort zone, you increase the likelihood of encountering serendipitous breakthroughs.

There is a Chinese proverb that beautifully captures this idea and I want to share it with you all. It is the story of Sāi Wēng Shī Mǎ.

Sāi Wēng lived on the border and raised horses for a living. One day, he lost one of his prized horses. When his neighbour heard of this misfortune, they came to comfort him. But Sāi Wēng simply asked, 'How could we know it is not a good thing for me?'

After some time, the lost horse returned, bringing with it another beautiful horse. The neighbour congratulated Sāi Wēng on his good fortune, but once again, he replied, 'How could we know it is not a bad thing for me?' And sure enough, one day, Sāi Wēng's son went for a ride on the new horse, only to be violently thrown off and break his leg.

The neighbour expressed their condolences, but Sāi Wēng calmly said, 'How could we know it is not a good thing for me?' As fate would have it, one year later, the Emperor's army arrived in the village to recruit all able-bodied men for war. Sāi Wēng's son was spared from certain death because of his injury.

The moral of the story? Do not rush to judgement, because misfortune often hides a silver lining, and what may initially appear as good luck can turn out to be misfortune in disguise. Many often attribute other people's fortunes to good luck, while their own misfortunes are the result of bad luck. It is 100 per cent true that some people are born with advantages and events happen to us that are outside our control. However, you can always do something to build upon what you have. Life is like a game of cards, and while we cannot control every card we are dealt, we can control how we play the game. We make our own luck. As much as that sentence might not sit well with you, it is true.

No one is inherently lucky or unlucky. It is all a matter of perspective. Some of the worst moments or periods in our lives often turn out to be pivotal turning points for the better. Looking back now, we would not change a thing, even though we would have done anything to change the situation in the moment. I was the unluckiest man in the world when I was 20; I broke my leg and ankle, was in a wheelchair for a year, lost my career, was depressed, etc. Now, I am the luckiest man in the world, as I would not be sitting on my balcony writing this sentence you are now reading if that unfortunate (or fortunate) accident had not happened.

Sometimes it is about finding the silver lining in the darkest of clouds. A setback or disappointment can be the catalyst for growth and resilience. No meaningful growth or transformation ever comes without some pain or suffering. The challenge might lead us to reevaluate our priorities, discover hidden strengths or even redirect our path toward something more meaningful. Just like Sāi Wēng, we can question the apparent misfortune and consider that there might be a greater purpose behind it.

OK, so we now know that luck is not just a random occurrence. In reality, it often follows those who are prepared, those who are scanning the horizon for opportunities and those who take action. Luck favours the persistent, the proactive, and the ones who are not afraid to seize opportunities and make a few mistakes along the way. Of course, embracing the concept of making our own luck definitely does not mean we dismiss the role of chance entirely. There will always be factors beyond our control. However, by focusing on what we can control – our actions, attitudes and choices – we can tilt the odds in our favour.

Remember, luck is not something that happens to us; it is something we create. So, I have one question for you: 'Do you feel lucky? Well, do ya, punk?'

Which makes you feel most energetic? Three hours on a packed plane, breathing in some hefty, sweaty gentleman's body odour and listening to what must be a teething baby while being contorted in an economy seat? Or an afternoon spent walking in the countryside, with the sun kissing your skin, the breeze at your back and the sound of trees moving in the wind?

You are a product of your environment. We have all heard this phrase before, but have we truly grasped its depth? It's not just about the physical spaces we inhabit. There's value in developing a heightened sense of awareness and sensitivity to the impact of your environments and the need to become ruthless about upgrading the quality of them. Tim Bunch's thinking regarding environments really resonated with me and I am excited to share the concept with you.

Physical environment: When we think of environments, our first instinct is to consider our physical surroundings. This includes our living or working spaces, the inside of our car, the clothes we wear and even the devices we use. Creating a clean and organized physical environment can have a profound effect on our mindset and productivity. I consider Marie Kondo[110] to be the authority on creating an energetic, aesthetic and motivating physical environment, so what do we do to create a quality office/desk environment that 'sparks joy'?

Tip 1: Set intentions. Want a promotion, or to start a side hustle? Keep these goals front of mind as you configure your workspace and you will feel inspired to design a space that will allow you to work toward and achieve those lofty ambitions of yours.

Tip 2: Discard what you do not need. Time to throw out those seven-year-old receipts and anything that is not needed. Clutter, be gone. If the item is sentimental, express gratitude and let it go; donate where possible.

Tip 3: Consolidate everything. Marie wants us to keep all similar items together. This helps us to know what we have and save over-ordering, saving a bit of money in the process and more importantly time spent looking for things. How many pens does one person need anyway? I counted and I had 38 – anyone want one?

Tip 4: Gather key supplies. When you are working, you want to be working, right? Make sure you have everything you need to hand, ensuring that you can focus, make the most of your working day and not need to work late. I see so many people who moan about long hours, but are constantly running around not doing anything. No thanks.

Tip 5: Add joy. You knew this one was coming. Marie recommends placing one item on your desk that is bound to spark joy, be it a small trinket, plant or vase of flowers. What is something small that makes you smile? Yeah, that. I have Nan's old bedside clock.

Body environment: You are what you eat. Eat crap, feel crap. Simple. Our physical bodies are perhaps the most important of the environments. We either make a small amount of time for our physical health today, or we will pay later. Taking care of our health through exercise and proper nutrition greatly impacts our overall wellbeing, productivity and creativity. Regular physical activity and a balanced diet can do wonders for our energy levels and mental clarity. It's 2 pm and you are flagging big time, you have a 1–1 in 30 minutes with your boss – what snack should you reach for? Nuts, bananas, oranges, coffee, oatmeal and chia seeds are just some of the snacks that will boost your energy.

Memetic environment: Our memetic environment comprises all the information we consume, such as books, podcasts, news and online content. It is crucial to be mindful of the quality of information we expose ourselves to – see Chapter 4, 'Breaking news', for more on this. Just as we consider the food we put in our mouths, we need to consider the information we consume, as it shapes our thoughts, beliefs and actions. I personally limit my news intake, avoid doom scrolling like the plague (it always makes me feel awful) and do not engage with negativity online, which I am now exposed to fairly regularly through my work. It is toxic – nothing good comes from going there. Nothing. I would rather engage with positive, energetic people who appreciate what I do and want to make a difference.

Spiritual environment: While spirituality is often associated with religion, it can also encompass a broader sense of something greater than ourselves. Whether it's finding solace in nature or exploring philosophical ideas, nurturing our spiritual environment helps keep us grounded and connected to something beyond our immediate concerns, which can be all-encompassing in the digital world. My younger brother finds his solace in the ocean and surfs all year round. In the UK, I might add, not Hawaii. Guess he heeds his own advice about there being no bad weather.

Financial environment: Our financial situation is an environment that can cause significant stress; in fact, financial pressure is the leading cause of stress outside the workplace for 37 per cent of us.[111] Improving our financial environment requires careful planning and smart choices and is often the environment that most of us want to improve – see Chapter 50, 'Show me the money', for more on financial wellbeing.

Relationship environment: The people you surround yourself with can transform your career, for better or worse. They can either uplift you or drain your energy. Toxic relationships and negative influences hold us back, while positive and supportive connections can fuel our growth. Surround yourself with people who inspire and motivate you, and do not feel guilty about distancing yourself from those who drain your energy – see Chapter 30, 'Your circle'.

In her book *Broadcasting Happiness*, Michelle Gielan dedicates an entire chapter to this topic, in what she describes as a strategic retreat:

> A retreat may be cowardly, but a strategic retreat is courageous and can help create conditions for a better relationship later on. Strategic retreats have long been used to win battles. In this sense, one can use it to defeat the ill effects of someone else's toxicity. A strategic retreat allows you the chance to regroup and reenter the fray stronger than ever.[112]

When you remove toxic people from your life, you will be shocked at how much energy you gain. It's like the weight of the world is lifted from your shoulders.

Network environment: Our network extends beyond our immediate relationships to include the communities and tribes we participate in; this is the extension of the relationship network. With the power of the internet, we can shape our network by following influential and inspiring individuals online. Engaging with like-minded people in our areas of interest can expand our knowledge and provide opportunities for growth. For me, LinkedIn has been this environment – I have met and curated a network of incredible humans who want to change the world and inspire me daily. Yours does not have to be on LinkedIn; it could be Instagram, your colleagues, volunteer networks, etc.

Natural environment: Consider two different breaths: one on the metro and one in the park – which energizes you more? Nature is the environment that in my opinion we overlook the most. Spending time outdoors, whether through outdoor hobbies like surfing or hiking or simply taking a short walk, has immense benefits for our physical, mental and emotional health. See Chapter 13, 'Want some green?', for more.

Self environment: Our self environment encompasses our personality, strengths, weaknesses and everything that makes us who we are. Practices like therapy, coaching and self-reflection can and do lead to personal growth and development; this is often the hardest to do, but often the most transformational. Trust me.

Upgrading and organizing our environments is a continuous process that requires awareness, intention and action. By making deliberate choices and taking steps to improve each environment, we will create a supportive, motivating and empowering ecosystem that enhances our sense of wellbeing and helps us thrive regardless of the external environment. All of our environments are interconnected and some will need more focus and work than others.

If I'm honest with myself and you, I could focus a bit more on my 'self' and 'spirituality' environments. Which would you benefit from working on?

Do you think that a promotion, bigger house or lottery win will make you happy in the long run? Or that bereavement, injury, trauma make you sadder over the same period? For sure, you will experience a spike in happiness or sadness. I've experienced both spikes recently – happiness caused by having recently completed a TEDx talk (which has been a dream for years) and sadness from the sudden death of my nan, which happened just two weeks beforehand.

We all have a tendency to believe that external factors like a new car, attractive partners or even the new iPhone will bring us lasting happiness. I will be happy when… And sure, they might give us a temporary boost of happiness. I mean, who would not be ecstatic about a sudden windfall or a significant life upgrade? However, over time, we tend to return to our baseline level of happiness. It's like gravity pulling us back to our emotional equilibrium. Welcome to the hedonic treadmill (also known as hedonic adaptation); time to take a spin and explore what it is to be happy. Actually happy.

According to the renowned happiness researcher, Sonja Lyubomirsky, our happiness set point is a combination of genetics, circumstances beyond our control and the part we can actually do something about, which is around 40 per cent to be exact. In her book, *The How of Happiness*, Sonja shares that 50 per cent of our happiness is set by genetics,

10 per cent is based on external factors and the remaining 40 per cent is left for us to adjust ourselves.[113] However, since then, she has acknowledged that while her original estimations of happiness's set point values were off, the core idea remains: we can control a degree of our own happiness. So, while we may not have complete control over our happiness and a lot is out of our hands, we do have some say in it.

We often reach for hedonic pleasures when we need a pick me up; something like an extra slice of cheesecake or a few glasses of wine, hoping to find some relief from the day we have had – 'oh what a day'. But as we all know too well, the high is fleeting and leaves you feeling empty and wanting more and before you know it, you are back to where you started, craving the next hit of pleasure. And the treadmill keeps running and running.

But fear not, there is a way to break free from this exhausting cycle, to step off the treadmill. Instead of solely relying on hedonic pleasures and quick fixes to get us through the day, we could perhaps consider incorporating some eudaimonic elements into our lives. Eudaimonia, remember, is a fancy word for finding deeper meaning and purpose; it can be a game changer in our pursuit of lasting happiness or joy, which is deeper and longer lasting. See Chapter 34, 'Happiness vs joy', for more.

It can be quite overwhelming though, all of this wellbeingness and trying to be good every day. No one is as good as they appear. I am certainly not and I fall short constantly. I like to think of it this way: you wake up each day with a blank canvas in front of you. Yesterday's successes or failures? Forget about them. Today is a fresh start, a chance to make progress, no matter how small. Every day, you start fresh. You get to decide how you fill the canvas of your day.

Will you paint it with a vibrant palette of positivity, self-care and a splash of joy? Or will you splatter it with negativity of past mistakes and unrealistic expectations?

Life throws curveballs and we end up face-planting into a metaphorical pile of you know what time and time again. Other times we feel like superheroes, smashing our goals and walking on water. But here is the secret: neither extreme defines us. It is about finding the middle ground, cutting ourselves some slack and celebrating the little victories.

Perfection? Nah, that's overrated. Progress is what matters. Maybe you can't tackle a full-hour workout or stick to your strict diet plan, but you can take a small step forward. Go easy on the mayo, add a bit more movement to your day instead. Remember, small changes make a big difference over time.

I recently injured my back and ended up in hospital. I had to take a month off from the gym and I was worried about losing all the progress I had made. But instead of dwelling on what I could not do, I focused on what I could do. I committed to taking 10,000 steps every day and you know what? When I finally returned to the gym, I was amazed to find that there was zero change in my body composition. Zero! It just goes to show that consistency in small efforts can keep us on track, even during setbacks. Blank. Canvas.

You ate too much yesterday, or you spent the day on the couch – forget about it. Forget about past mistakes or shortcomings. Be kind to yourself and embrace what you can do today. I had an eight-year battle with bulimia and would ruminate on any little slip-up, beating myself up for days. I am only human and I do what I can. Same for you. So trust me, I know it's tempting to fall into the trap of self-criticism or excessive self-praise. Life is a delicate balance and happiness lies in finding that middle ground. And remember, it is often fleeting and happiness returns to its baseline, so soon you won't be bothered anyway.

So, what can we do about it?

Tip 1: You are only human. You will get it wrong again and again. No worries, this makes you human. Learn to accept the inevitable emotions that arise when you 'get it wrong', as rejecting them leads to anger and frustration. I have struggled with this for years and am working on it every day.

Tip 2: Shifting perspective. Recognize that external factors, such as material possessions or hedonic pleasures, provide only fleeting happiness. Shift your focus from chasing short-lived highs to cultivating lasting joy (eudaimonia) – see Chapter 34. This will look different for everyone. I need to make/protect more time for hobbies that are not work related, one being my Spanish practice.

Tip 3: Relationships. We can all increase the effort that we put into our relationships. Like plants, they will wither without care and attention. Go on a date with your significant other, go to the pub with some friends or spend more time talking to your children. There is nothing more important than this.

Tip 4: Perfection is a myth. Release the need for perfection and celebrate progress, regardless of how minuscule. Maybe you overspent this month, it's not the end of the world – learn from it and start again fresh at payday. We could all do with embracing a little more self-compassion and celebrating the little victories along the way.

Tip 5: The attitude of ambivalence. Go easy on the self-criticism and also watch out for excessive self-praise. What happened yesterday is now in the past; learn what you can, smile and start again today. Blank canvas.

Tip 6: Gratitude. At the same time every day write down three things you are grateful for. Even if you have had the WORST day at work, you will be amazed that you will always be able to find three things that you are grateful for, some little slithers of happiness. Maybe the sun that shone through the clouds on the way home from the train, a colleague who complimented your trainers and getting to inbox zero at 17.25. Eventually you will begin to see and appreciate these moments throughout the day even before you get to this exercise.

So, focus on the little things, focus on what brings you joy, focus on grabbing a massive slice of cheesecake while you are there. Because tomorrow, we start fresh.

44
CHILDLIKE WONDER

Being called childlike may sound like an insult to some, but I take it as a compliment. Good job really, as I do get called childish with a fair amount of regularity. I guess that will happen when you do videos on the toilet like I do! There is a significant difference between being childlike and being childish: while childlike behaviour allows us to see the world with wide eyes and a sense of curiosity, being childish on the other hand involves seeking instant gratification and demanding guarantees for everything.

Recently, it was my nephew Fergus's third birthday, and I witnessed first-hand the pure excitement and curiosity that comes with being a child. Every new word, song or animal noise is an adventure to him. We ran down to the sea together, filled a bucket up and spent hours putting the water gun to good use. Fergus found deep enjoyment in spraying Grandad and Uncle Clive when they least expected it, giggling every single time. I enjoyed it almost as much as Fergus did, until he got me. 'Naughty Fergus.' It got me thinking: as adults, how can we reintroduce surprise, curiosity, childlike wonder and a bit of fun back into our lives? Oh, and I am not talking about organized fun, as great as that is…

Tip 1: Put it down. We have already spoken about this, but we are going there again. Our smartphones are a constant source of distraction, draining every available moment of our time and attention. When was the last time you waited in a queue without checking your phone? Seriously. We are so consumed that we often miss out on the little moments of joy and wonder happening around us. Not long ago I was so engrossed in my phone walking through the park near home that I completely missed a family of ducks waddling right past me. It was only when a nearby child's excited laughter caught my attention that I looked up and saw the adorable sight. Lesson learned: real-life ducks are way more entertaining than Instagram ducks.

Tip 2: Get outside. Who remembers the game of dropping a stick off one side of a bridge upstream and running to the other side to see it float past? Just me? Sure. What about seeing a massive pile of leaves and being compelled to run into them and kick them around? Surely you did this one. Anyways, leaves and sticks are not just for kids; nature has a way of captivating and enriching us all. Take a closer look at the intricate patterns on a flower petal, marvel at the graceful flight of a butterfly or listen to the soothing sound of leaves rustling in the wind. Ask yourself one question: What would Fergus do?' That's right, kick the leaves.

Tip 3: Slow it down. It is the easiest thing in the world to get caught up in the hustle and bustle of daily life. We rush from one task to another, rarely taking a moment to pause and appreciate the little things that bring us joy. Slow down for a second. Notice the small details that often go unnoticed: the warmth of a morning cup of coffee, the vibrant colours of a sunset, the warmth of the sun or the laughter of a loved one – especially Uncle Kevin's. These moments are what life is all about. Last week the train was late; I was in a rush and feeling stressed. As I hurried to the office, a sudden downpour caught me off guard. Instead of getting frustrated, I laughed and decided to slow down and embrace the moment. You can't get wetter than wet, so why worry? I was 'wetter than an otter's pocket' by the time I got to the office but I didn't care, and nor did anyone else.

Tip 4: Who says games are only for kids? We could all do with injecting some playfulness into our daily routines by turning mundane tasks into fun challenges. Almost anything can be turned into a game if you try hard enough. Working at your desk – how long can you stand on one leg for? Going to get coffee? Race down the stairs against the lift. I could go on. What have you got to lose but boredom itself?

Tip 5: Break the routine. As adults, we often get stuck in routines and follow the same patterns day after day. Same journey to work, same desk, same times for breaks; the monotony rolls on until we retire at 68. While routines provide us with structure and efficiency, as we have discussed throughout the book, they can also dampen and pretty much eliminate any remaining shreds of spontaneity and curiosity. Break free from the monotony by trying something new and unexpected. Take a different route to work – one day I would like to paddleboard down the Thames to the office, cook Eritrean food for dinner, try a new hobby. I have said for ages that I want to learn how to dance – I need to just do it. By breaking away from the predictable, you open yourself up to new experiences and opportunities. Laurie Santos, Yale professor and creator of the wildly successful 'Science of Wellbeing' course, shared with *GQ* that 'Novel stimuli tend to activate regions of our brain that are associated with rewards; as well as our attention ... you are more likely to notice things and be present. There is lots of evidence that simply being more present can improve our mood and happiness.'[114]

Tip 6: Dream. Children have limitless imaginations and dream big without constraints. When I was younger, I wanted to be a bishop, which is odd as we were not a church-going family. I always was an odd kid, I think I liked the hat. As adults, we have to be practical and rational; we have jobs and bills to pay so we set aside our dreams and aspirations. But why should we? Allow yourself to dream big again, indulge yourself for even for a while. Whether it is starting that side hustle of yours, learning a musical instrument or travelling to your dream destination, give yourself permission to dream – it costs nothing. While I was doing the Camino de Santiago (walking 860 km across Spain), I met Les, a 78-year-old man from Australia who was on his 10th Camino and walking faster than I was. You are capable of more than you give yourself credit for. Whether you think you can, or you think you cannot, you are probably right. Back to Mary Schmich's address to the Class of '97 in the *Chicago Tribune*, 'Sunscreen': 'Don't feel guilty if you don't know what you want to do with your life... the most interesting people I know didn't know at 22 what they wanted to do with their lives, some of the most interesting 40-year-olds I know still don't.'[115]

Tip 7: Stage a funtervention. Sit down with your colleagues and ask yourselves, Do we have time for fun this week?' Work doesn't have to be boring. If you're sitting there, scratching your collective heads, then you need to get to work. It could be as simple as choosing a word of the week, which you have to use in meetings – try squeezing 'rambunctious' or 'raspberry swirl' into your next sales call – or counting the number of times that the COO says 'culture' during the all hands.

Being a big kid does not mean being childish, it means being childlike, embracing joy, curiosity and a sense of wonder in our adult lives. By putting our phones down, getting outside, slowing down, making things a game, breaking away from routines and dreaming big, we can reintroduce childlike wonder into our lives.

So, the next time you find yourself caught up in the seriousness of life and adulthood, take a moment to ask yourself, 'What would Fergus do?'

It's 12.30 pm and you're sitting at your desk – are you eating al fresco or al desko? Prior to the pandemic, almost a third of workers in the UK were guilty of eating their meals at their desks[116] and one can only assume that this statistic has worsened since then. It certainly seems that way, as in 2021 it was found that over 62 per cent of US workers said they eat lunch at their desks.[117] But is this really the way we want to be spending our lunch breaks? Are we more productive this way? Happier? Healthier?

I'm going to do something that most British people do not like to do. I'm going to take a moment to compare ourselves in a negative light to the French. The average worker in the UK now takes just 34 minutes for their lunch break with over half of workers (52 per cent) skipping it completely.[118] While in France, 43 per cent of French respondents took 45 minutes or more for lunch, the average lunch break being 54 minutes[119] and 72 per cent ate at a restaurant at least once a week.[120] If we found ourselves in a French office and hordes were sitting at their desks scarfing down sorry-looking salads and sandwiches like we do in the UK, the company would be fined for breaking the law. 'Allez les Bleus.' I mean, 'Swing Low, Sweet Chariot.'

Now, I know a strong work ethic is admirable. However, if you believe that you can be productive for eight or more hours a day without taking a break, I'm sorry to burst your bubble, but you are straight-up wrong. Nobody can sustain such high levels of productivity without a modicum of rest or decent sustenance. Just take a look at the Pomodoro Technique, the world's most famous productivity technique. It recommends 25 minutes of focused work followed by a short break. Not eight hours straight – 19 times the recommended period.

If the productivity argument does not convince you, maybe my personal experience will. I have pretty severe back pain daily, which started during the 'work from home' times during the pandemic and which I have been unable to diagnose for over two years since. I believe it is from hunching over a desk with poor posture for years. Trust me, I wish I had stepped away more often to give my poor spine a break – see Chapter 7, 'The world's greatest stretch', to try to prevent these musculoskeletal issues before they arise. You do not want to end up like Quasimodo over here.

Maybe you can't get to the restaurant for lunch, but surely you can take a break and have a drink. Right? Sadly not. The great British tea-and-biscuit break is becoming a thing of the past, with 15 per cent of workers 'not allowed' to have one. A poll of 4,000 adults in employment found 7 in 10 take under 15 minutes of breaks (outside their lunch break) a day and 43 per cent take under 10 minutes.[121] Is this strictly a British problem? Nope. Replace the word tea with coffee and the stats may change a bit, but the diminishing break does not.

Tip 1: The great British tea break. I challenge you to block out at least 15 minutes in your calendar today at 4 pm and go for a cup of tea (or any other drink you prefer). The key is to step away from your screen and take a moment for yourself or with others. I was lucky enough to be made a cup of tea recently by the author of *The Art of Tea* himself, Steve Schwartz. Steve shared this with the group and it really resonated with me: 'The process and the ritual will have far greater lasting effects on the mind and body than simply the antioxidant properties within.' This whole process is less about the tea than it is the ritual of taking a break and being present for a minute. Slow everything down: taste, smell, feel, be. We must remember that we are not interfaces of machines. We are human beings who cannot and should not be plugged in all day long. It is time to step away from the desk, leave the phone, let that status dot go orange – the work will still be there when you get back. Trust me, nothing bad will happen, I promise.

Tip 2: Block it OOO. Block it out in your diary and then let your team know – do not send them the same calendar event, rather create another and tag it as 'free', so as to not block their diary out too. Bonus manager points if you do it for you and your team (provided that time works for all).

Tip 3: Team lunches. The best way to get out to lunch? Invite the team, the client, your boss along. That way you do not miss anything, as everyone is with you. Even better when work pays for lunch too – nothing better than free food.

So, who's heading out for lunch?

Why am I not a 22-year-old tech founder with washboard abs and a villa in Tahiti?' It doesn't take much time on social media until we start to ask ourselves these questions. Why the hell is everyone so good looking, while I feel like Frodo Baggins over here? I have more hair on my toes now than I do on my head.

Fear not, we are going to look east again for some advice; more specifically, to Japan and the ancient Japanese idiom of Oubaitori. Every year the four most well-known Japanese trees all come to bloom in spring: cherry blossoms, plum, peach and apricot. Each flower blooms in its own time and we're no different. We all grow and bloom at our own pace. It reminds us that everyone is on their own journey through life and we should focus on our own growth and try not to compare ourselves so much to others, celebrating our individuality and uniqueness. There is no rush whatsoever and you will get to where you need to be in your own time. Which tree are you? I definitely identify most with plum.

Social media, more often than not, leaves us feeling pretty rubbish, but is it any surprise when everyone is off living their best life and you are in back-to-back calls, working from the corner of your bedroom? These comparisons can leave us feeling empty, yet we still reach back into the digital cookie jar at every single opportunity we get. This is not your fault though; the odds are very much stacked against you. Even if you do not realize it, you are up against millions of the world's smartest people every single day. It really is David vs Goliath. David is your waning attention span and Goliath is an army of scientists, psychologists and UX designers fighting for every second of your attention. As we mentioned earlier, the average person checks their phone 352 times per day, spending over 7 hours on screens. If we did anything else that much, we would say we had a serious problem, right?

Therefore, whenever you manage to drag/divert your eyes away from the black mirror of your phone, television or computer, remember how much of a monumental victory that really is.

All of this makes you want to delete your socials, right? Not yet! Social media is very much a double-edged sword: it gives and it takes. According to Deloitte, 4 in 10 Gen Zs and Millennials feel lonely and inadequate due to using it. However, more than half of each generation say that accessing mental health resources has become easier because of social media and that social media has an overall positive impact on their lives, particularly given the ability to connect with friends, family and social causes.[122]

I know this first-hand. As I have already shared with you, over the past 13 years I have battled with depression, anxiety, bulimia and suicidal ideation. I felt broken, alone and fundamentally flawed. The thought of sharing my struggles seemed unimaginable. Then six years ago I mustered the courage to start sharing my story, piece by piece, at the occasional event. And guess what? I discovered that there were 10, 100, 1,000 people just like me, fighting their own battles. I was not alone. For years, it was only my mum who knew.

Four years ago I took the leap and started sharing my story on social media. I thought, if I can help one person, it will be worth it. The first few posts I agonized over, I wrote, re-wrote, re-wrote and re-wrote a bit more. To my surprise, when I finally posted, I found that there were 10,000, 100,000, 1,000,000 people who could relate to my experiences and this is all due to social media.

Here are a few ball bearings to load up for a shot at Goliath:

Tip 1: Celebrate others. When you see a colleague, friend or stranger achieve success, it is not a slight on you; don't lament your supposed 'lack of progress'. Remember the concept of Oubaitori; your time will come. Celebrate their achievements and soon they will be celebrating yours.

Tip 2: Set limits. You can set limits on your phone to limit your social media usage. This really does help, automating what we often struggle with. I take a rather simple approach to prevent me from using social media on the weekend – I just delete the apps and re-download Monday. Works for me.

Tip 3: Find your tribe. Find individuals and groups who inspire, celebrate and motivate you. You do not have to surround yourself with negative people online. Some you may have to tolerate as they are family, the rest you can choose. See Chapter 30, 'Your circle', for more.

Tip 4: Let's take this offline. While social media allows us to connect with a multitude of people, it is essential to nurture the relationships that matter offline too. Why not meet face to face over a cup of tea or coffee?

Tip 5: Curate the feed. Unfollow accounts that make you feel inadequate or trigger negative emotions. Surround yourself with content that inspires and uplifts you.

Tip 6: Reality check. Be kind to yourself. Do not compare your behind the scenes with someone else's highlight reel. You are enough, just as you are. Screw Pedro, his six pack and his holiday.

Social media has given me much angst, but it has given me much joy, having found my tribe of people who want to make a difference in the world. It is a tool that can unite and divide, it just depends how you want to wield the slingshot.

47

TOILET BREAK WELLBEING

Most wellbeing solutions do not improve wellbeing and may even worsen it.

2023 research from Oxford University Wellbeing Research Centre evaluated the effectiveness of the usual suite of wellbeing initiatives provided for individuals at work, such as wellbeing apps, mindfulness, relaxation products, coaching for wellbeing, wellbeing courses, volunteering and more.

It found that many of these initiatives do more harm than good from a mental wellbeing perspective, actually worsening individual subjective wellbeing.[123] Somewhat unsurprisingly, offering 'off-the-shelf' solutions will not provide a satisfactory solution to the systemic problems of working conditions and work-induced stress. There is very little evidence in support of any benefits from these interventions, despite a lot of noise to the contrary. Of the interventions measured, volunteering appeared to be the most beneficial. This is hardly surprising when we consider that belonging is one of the biggest drivers of positive wellbeing at work.[124]

Do I think these initiatives don't work at all? No, I don't, definitely not; rather, that they do not work if we don't also address the organizational challenges and stressors and consider how they may in fact exacerbate stress. If someone doesn't have five minutes to themselves, these well-meaning solutions will not and do not work. We need to first have a bit of time and space before even considering adding something else to our proverbial plates. As time is at a premium, we need to consider this in our efforts, to meet people where they are. If only there was something that we did eight times every day that we could attach positive habits to…

Wellbeing is often portrayed as this big, scary, incomprehensible subject that is either in complete crisis or so 'woo woo' that it engages no one. But guess what? It can be as simple as going to the toilet. Yes, you heard me right. Do you know how many times the average person goes to the toilet every day? About eight. That's eight opportunities to flush and flourish. Eight opportunities to flush and do something for yourself. If you think you don't go eight times every day, count tomorrow. You'll be surprised. I was.

This was where the concept of toilet break wellbeing was born. I am pretty sure the concept came to me while sitting on the throne, like all best ideas do. I started with a few selfies in the toilet and now I have a full ring light set up in my bathroom and I have to warn people when they come around that I don't, in fact, run an OnlyFans channel from my bathroom. I started toilet break wellbeing for two reasons: to make wellbeing more fun and engaging, sharing that small, smart wellbeing decisions with consistency over time = a radical difference; and secondly because when I was 25, I was so anxious that every time I left my front door I felt like I was going to wet myself and ended up wearing an adult diaper for almost a year (not that I ever needed it).

If we really think about it, most of what we perceive as problems will magically go away after a walk outside and a good night's sleep. We love to look for complex solutions, when it is often a simplistic solution that we need. It is tempting to inundate ourselves with books, videos, podcasts and articles in an effort to become happier and more productive, when the most obvious adjustments and improvements are often the most simple and straightforward. If you don't sleep enough or you eat terribly it doesn't matter what else you do, your mood will suck and you will struggle to control your negative emotions and lack energy and motivation. Simple, really.

Now, let's get back to the toilet. The toilet is no longer just for private business or taking a cheeky little 10 minutes away from work. We are going to stack some habits on top of your trip to the commode. OK, not while you are in progress – wash your hands first, please. For example, imagine doing 10 press-ups every time you visit the toilet this year – you would end up doing a whopping 29,200 press-ups! OK, maybe that is a bit extreme and may be slightly difficult to do in the middle of the office, but the point stands: small, achievable habits add up over time. Wellbeing is no small thing, but is made up of small things.

Here are a few things you could do after you flush. Keep in mind that other frequent trigger activities could work instead – like finishing a meeting or completing a task at work:

Tip 1: Breathe – try a few box breaths.

Tip 2: Stretch – try the world's greatest stretch.

Tip 3: Get some fresh air.

Tip 4: Read a few pages of a book or an article.

Tip 5: Tell someone how much you appreciate them.

Tip 6: Listen to a motivational song.

Tip 7: Clean your workspace – Marie Kondo would be proud.

Tip 8: Go for a walk – stretch those legs.

Tip 9: Or do nothing – shut your eyes and just be for a second.

Remember, wellbeing is not so much about grand gestures, big events or complicated programmes; it is about the accumulation of small, often simple and analogue actions/decisions over time.

Time to flush and flourish.

48

IN THE TUNNEL

We all have that one thing about ourselves that we just do not like to talk about; that thing that we don't even acknowledge or think about. The lucky ones among us have multiple things, like a huge pile of dirty laundry hidden in the corner of our minds. We avoid looking at it, acknowledging it or risking disturbing its fragile existence. Better to just ignore it. Someone else will deal with it. We will go to great lengths to distract ourselves from it, diving into careers, indulging in vices, immersing ourselves in activities, jetting off on travel adventures or seeking solace in relationships. Anything to keep that part of ourselves locked away, buried deep down.

But here's the thing: that little secret part of us, that dirty laundry we try to avoid, will never truly disappear. It lingers, casting a large shadow over our lives and affecting us in more ways than we can imagine. We cannot outrun it, we cannot hide from it, no matter how fast we sprint or how skillfully we evade it, because eventually we are going to need a new pair of pants.

I will use myself as the sacrificial guinea pig here to bring this point to life. However, please bear in mind that this is my experience and does not constitute medical advice. If you find yourself in a similar situation, please speak to a medical professional. I have, multiple times.

My parents split up when I was 13 and I sought solace in food. I would walk home from school and get four Snickers bars for £1 from the corner shop and they were all demolished before turning the corner to walk up to the house. It was a momentary relief, from what was a difficult period for that young man. I was overweight, unhappy and hated myself; I was an easy target to be bullied and the bullies did not disappoint. I did end up losing the weight, but the way I felt about myself remained – I loathed what I looked like. Obviously, I told no one any of this; I was the happy jovial 'big guy'. When I broke my leg and ankle at 19, all the weight was found again and I gained about 25 kg. After the most difficult year of my life, I gained the ability to walk again and began to lose weight. However, I developed bulimia in the process. Of course, I never told anyone until I nearly ended up in hospital. It was something I never thought a big rugby player like me would have to deal with. I hid it away, refusing to fully acknowledge it, fearing the judgement and shame that I believed would accompany it.

After a year, I told my mum and only because I had to. I was so calorie restricted (eating strictly chicken and broccoli) at this point that I was struggling to speak and I was sent home from work. I didn't tell another soul for four years and fought with the illness for another seven years. About six years ago, I began to open up, telling close friends and family, eventually small safe spaces at work, and now I share with pretty much anyone who will listen. The first time was and will always be the hardest, and it has been easier at every single telling since. I am not the largest, leanest, lightest, but I am the happiest I have ever been in my own skin and what was once my biggest shame is now my fire; it sustains me and will be one of the reasons that I will engage a billion people in the betterment of wellbeing.

Why am I telling you this?

Here is what I have learned: secrecy and shame thrive in darkness. It gains power when we keep it hidden, festering in the corners of our minds. The moment we find the courage to acknowledge it, to speak about it, its power begins to diminish. It is as if we have turned on a light in that dark tunnel we have been trapped in.

Back to my brother Scott, who once shared with me something that has stuck with me. He told me that when the Royal Marines land in the night, they create a perimeter around the helicopter. I thought, yeah ok, makes sense, they're protecting the helicopter. Nope. They all wait patiently in the pitch black, allowing their eyes to adjust to the darkness. It does not take long until the darkness becomes their light.

That is a lesson that we can apply to our own lives. When we find ourselves trapped in the tunnel of life (every person's tunnel is different), surrounded by darkness, fear, loneliness, with the desperate desire to escape, it is the most natural thing in the world to want to sprint as fast as we can to the exit. I would have done almost anything for most of my life to have been someone else. But what happens if we muster the courage to stay in the darkness just a bit longer? What if we resist the urge to run and allow our eyes to adjust to the darkness?

The darkest periods of our lives can and often do become our greatest sources of light, warmth, hunger, fire, passion. You get it. They shape us, teach us and fuel our growth. It may be tough right now, but trust me, the light will shine again. You will emerge from that tunnel stronger, wiser and better equipped to navigate whatever is thrown in your path next.

As dark and as lonely, scary and perilous the tunnel may feel, please know that you are not alone in this journey. We all have our tunnels to traverse, our darkness to confront, our own piles of dirty laundry. But by opening up when we are good and ready, by sharing our struggles, seeking support from others, we can and will find solace and strength in each other's experiences. Remember, a problem shared is a problem halved. Damn right.

No tips for this one, team. Just remember, even the toughest people on planet earth, the Royal Marines, need time to adjust to the darkness. It may not feel like it now, but one day it will be your light. 'This too shall pass.' You got this.

What metrics have you adopted to measure and track your wellbeing? Steps, resting heartbeat, meditation streaks? Are they helping or actually harming you?

If you measure anything with regard to your wellbeing, I am sure that on more than one occasion you have found yourself obsessing over a specific goal. I have regularly obsessed over making sure I hit 10,000 steps per day. Which has been widely touted as the number to aim for. Sound familiar?

Confession time, I have been more than a little obsessive and unforgiving with the 10K over the past few years. When I got my first Fitbit in 2018, I became determined to meet that magical number without fail. No ifs, no buts, no maybes. I even walked on days when I was sick, or when I should have been enjoying quality time with loved ones. The odd time I did fall short, the guilt was pretty spectacular. I would ruminate on it for days.

My intention was good, my underlying goal was always health; yet my non-compromising attitude towards that goal became unhealthy. It took me some time to realize that my wellbeing is about so much more than a single or bunch of metrics – I do see the irony in this, given what I do for a living. So, in 2023, I decided to soften my approach, loosening the target. I have proudly missed the 10,000 steps goal quite a few times and guess what? The world is still spinning.

When it comes to wellbeing data, or any data in fact, be cautious of the solitary statistic; it provides us with one very small part of the holistic picture. A great example being that if you want to lose weight and simply focus on the number on the scales, it would probably be beneficial to start smoking, as having a cigarette can satiate hunger. Not that I need to say this, but please do not do that. To truly develop a deep, nuanced, rich and holistic understanding of our health and wellbeing, we need to consider the context and question what other information is needed.

It is called data manipulation for a reason. If you want a statistic to support an argument that we should all fly dragons to work to save the environment, I am sure you could find one. If you look hard enough, you can find a data point to support just about anything. 'It is easy to obtain confirmations, or verifications, for nearly every theory – if we look for confirmations' – Karl Popper, who is widely recognized as one of the greatest philosophers of the 21st century.[125]

Fun fact: back in the late 19th century, prior to the discovery of blood types in 1901, giving people blood transfusions was a risky procedure. In order to get around the need to transfuse others with blood, some doctors resorted to using a blood substitute. That substitute was milk. Yep, milk. It went pretty much how you would expect it to. They were working from data that said the minute oil and fatty particles found in milk would be turned into white blood cells.[126] Makes sense to me. I'm AB semi-skimmed+.

So, there is a distinction to make here, a distinction between data, information and knowledge. Data is simply raw facts and figures without any context. It is just the beginning, like a solitary puzzle piece. Information is processed data that has been given some meaning and context; it is the puzzle coming together at the edges, revealing a clearer picture. Knowledge takes it one step further; we go beyond comprehension and apply the information in a practical and meaningful way, connecting the dots and generating new understanding and insight.

So team, who is up for moving from wellbeing data to wellbeing knowledge?

Tip 1: Embrace the holistic. Wellbeing is about so much more than just about physical health; it encompasses mental, emotional, social and even financial wellbeing. When exploring wellbeing data, consider the bigger picture and explore how different factors interact. Maybe you are smashing the steps, but how are your relationships as a result?

Tip 2: With a pinch of salt. Metrics are very helpful tools, but they do not define your self-worth or happiness. I know it's not easy, but try not to get caught up in chasing a single number or goal. Instead, focus on cultivating a more balanced, nuanced perspective. It's hard, but it's worth it.

Tip 3: Context is king. Remember that data without context is basically useless. Look beyond the surface statistics and explore the underlying factors, circumstances and influences to develop information and knowledge. Resting heart rate is up. Why is that? Ahh, I slept three hours last night. Maybe I'll start there.

Tip 4: Personalization. Everyone's wellbeing journey is different; try to avoid comparing yourself and your metrics to others. It's like comparing apples and oranges – sure, they are both fruits, but they are not similar.

Tip 5: Technology vs intuition. While technology and wearables provide valuable insights, you still know best. Trust your gut and listen to your intuition. If you need a day off, take a day off – leave the smart watch at home.

Tip 6: Experiment and iterate. What worked for you five years ago is probably not suitable today and it definitely will not be in five years' time. Don't be afraid to try different approaches, experiment with new strategies and shake things up. If things don't change, that's when you need to worry.

Tip 7: Celebrate progress, not perfection. Wellbeing is not something that is achieved or failed overnight – rather over a lifetime. Acknowledge and celebrate the small wins. You hit your step goal for four out of seven days – nice work.

50

SHOW ME THE MONEY

It seems to be one thing after another at the moment, doesn't it? We've all been through an extremely challenging time over the past few years and it seems as if we're always in for more stormy weather, especially with regard to our finances. This, coupled with the fact that most of us didn't learn the basics around money at school, compounds the problem even further, with personal finances now being the biggest driver of stress outside of the workplace.[127]

We are all in this same financial storm together; however, we are certainly not all in the same boat. Some of us are safe and sound in the life raft, while others are hanging on to a floating door. The lucky few will sail through relatively unaffected while the majority of us will have to work even harder in our rowing boats and some are just about keeping their heads above water. It is more important than ever that we recognize and address this.

I don't pretend to be a financial wellbeing expert; however, Ryan Briggs is the Founder of FinWELL and is on a mission to smash the stigma that remains around this topic and help us all talk about money.

The biggest challenge for Ryan and his team was to come up with a framework that could help everyone, regardless of age, background, demographic, job role, level of income, savings, experience, confidence, etc. Not an easy challenge, but I think he has done a pretty stellar job.

He shared with me a super simple, four-step guide called the PAWA (Power) Plan. Yes, it is spelled incorrectly, as it worked for the acronym. Each of the four letters of PAWA represent a step and we start with the P for your Personal Money Score:

Personal Money Score (P). Like any area of wellbeing, we need a method for measuring and tracking our progress, and it is certainly no different with your financial wellbeing. If you treasure it, measure it. There are five key elements to financial wellbeing that we will be assessing and scoring together, with 1 being the lowest score and 10 being the best it can be:

1 *Money confidence.* First up is your general confidence when it comes to managing money. Twenty-four million UK adults don't feel confident managing their money,[128] but why is this? Most of us did not learn the basics around money at school, so we enter adulthood and often have to learn from our own mistakes. I know I certainly have. I was in debt until I was 27, maxing out credit cards every single month. Unless we had a parent, guardian or someone else to look up to and learn from, most of us have never learned about debt and credit, how to budget, how to spend sensibly and how to build up emergency funds for the unexpected.

2 *Relationship with money.* We all have one, some are healthier than others, and like all relationships, it changes over time and needs ongoing work. Ryan told me that our relationship with money is actually ingrained in us by the age of seven. A scary thought. There are many things that contribute to our relationship with money, such as how much of it we had growing up, was money spoken about openly at home or was it a source of stress, did you receive pocket money, etc? All these things ultimately contribute to us forming our attitudes, beliefs, behaviours, habits and decisions when it comes to money.

3 *Ability to pay bills.* This one is fairly straightforward to understand. This is about being able to cover your committed outgoings and get through the month without having to dip into the dreaded overdraft. Which is a monthly occurrence for a lot of people.

4 *Financial resilience.* Do you have a fund for unexpected bills, costs or emergencies? According to a survey by the Money and Pensions Service, around a quarter of UK adults (11.5 million people) have less than £100 in their savings account, with one in six people having no savings at all.[129] How many months would you be able to survive if all income stopped tomorrow? But how much is enough? This is, of course, different for everyone. You first need to work out your committed monthly outgoings such as mortgage/rent payments, bills, food and essential travel. Next step, we start to save what we can, aiming for three to six months, which is a really healthy position to be in.

5 *Future plans.* This is where most of us fall down, as it is hard to visualize what we might need to achieve our desired lifestyles and goals. How much are you going to need, confident you will get near that figure? This includes pensions, investments, etc.

Rank yourself from 1–10 on each of these five key elements. Add up your scores and double it to give yourself a score out of 100. No need to fret, we will look to make improvements together.

Areas of Focus (A). Now, there is definitely a lot to think or worry about when it comes to money and it can seem complex, confusing and more than a bit overwhelming. Time to focus on five key areas. You can choose which is more relevant to you and move through them at your own pace:

- *Money mindset and management.* This includes your relationship with money, dealing with debt, basic budgeting, spending habits and building financial resilience with emergency funds.

- *The property ladder.* This is a world full of jargon, from fixed-term mortgages to flexible interest rates. Some will want to take out their first mortgage, others to reduce the size, find the best deals, buy-to-lets, work towards becoming mortgage free or releasing equity.

- *Protecting what is important.* Protecting your income, family and future. This could include income protection, life insurance, critical illness cover, wills, LPAs (lasting powers of attorney) or tax and estate planning – making things easier for loved ones, were the worst to happen.

- *Investing for the future.* Establishing short-, medium- and long-term goals and understanding ways to save and invest your money tax efficiently, exploring/ defining your risk tolerance. There is no need to become any type of investment guru – Warren Buffet you are not. However, it is important to understand that you are already an investor if you have a workplace pension and you owe it to yourself to maximize those returns.

- *Modern retirement planning.* Understanding the options available, ensuring you have enough money in later life to do the things that make you happy, make sure that it lasts and pass it onto your loved ones as tax efficiently as possible.

What are your next steps? (W) Now that you have your (P)ersonal money score and your (A)reas of focus, you are well on your way to getting your PAWA. You will need to understand the difference between financial education, financial guidance and financial advice and then decide what stage you are at and what is right for you:

1 *Education*. A lot of people will want to improve their knowledge, understanding and confidence around their areas of focus, so will need to access trusted and reputable educational content. This can include videos, articles, guides, reports, infographics and podcasts depending on how you like to learn and consume information.

2 *Guidance*. Some will then want to talk about money in a group or on a 1–1 basis. This gives you a chance to engage and interact with others, to share your own needs, goals or challenges and be guided or signposted to relevant resources, which will help you take your financial wellbeing to the next level.

3 *Advice*. Some will require professional advice, which involves sharing more information around your personal situation with a qualified professional, who can make personal recommendations that may include specific products or solutions.

Taking action (A). The last and possibly most important step to get your PAWA is to feel empowered and take action! I know, you have what feels like 24 minutes spare per week, but the best thing you can do is to allocate some time and commit to focusing/working on your PAWA plan and improving that score.

Bonus tip: The tried-and-tested 'accountabilabuddy'. Buddy up with a friend, family member or work colleague to continue the conversation, ask each other questions and keep each other accountable.

Ryan told me that 'the one thing more important than our ability to earn money, is our attitude towards and relationship with it'. By building a healthy relationship with your money, you'll be able to navigate out of any financial storm.

I took this chapter title from a track by house music legend, Danny Tenaglia, featuring Celeda – check it out if you haven't heard it before. Where our wellbeing is concerned, there may be more truth in this statement than we might believe at first glance. There is a whole host of academic research on the positive impact music can have on our brains and mental wellbeing. Put your favourite track on now and you will experience this for yourself. As I write this, I'm shuffling between *The Last Samurai* soundtrack by Hans Zimmer and Rufus du Sol's latest album. As I was planning this chapter, I thought to myself, 'To do this chapter justice, I need to chat to someone.' I found just the person too: DJ, wellbeing veteran and founder of Harmonizing the Mind, Rob Stephenson. Here is what came out of our conversation together…

Did you know that over 90 per cent of us listen to music regularly? I didn't. That's over 7 billion humans. In the United States, they spend more than 25 hours each week jamming out to their favourite tunes.[130] That's a lot of time. While our music tastes are as personal and individual as we are, this is one area where many of us can find common ground. As the world and the places where we interact online become more and more polarized and full of hate, music can be the glue that connects us to each other and to our shared histories.

Think of your favourite movie. Think about a scene that you remember well. One that features some music. Now try to think what that scene would feel like if the music was taken away. It would suck all emotion out of the movie. Imagine Darth Vader marching along to silence; the runners in *Chariots of Fire* without the score from Vangelis; or *The Godfather* without that iconic theme tune by Nino Rota. Music adds to the emotion and in some cases is the primary agitator. I'm personally a huge fan of the work of Hans Zimmer and Christopher Nolan, such as *Interstellar* and Christian Bale's *Batman* films. We all have soundtracks to our lives. Music that reminds us of periods and phases. Collectively, we often take this for granted and fail to realize that music plays such an important role in our lives.

Having suffered with back pain, my ears perked up when Rob told me about one study involving patients who experience fibromyalgia. They found that listening to music for just an hour per day reduced the perception of pain in the participants. Furthermore, it also resulted in lower incidences of associated anxiety and depression in the patients as compared to a control group:[131]

Tip 1: Musical therapy. If you, like me, experience pain regularly, think about scheduling some time each day to listen to positive music that you enjoy. Another fabulous music-related study measured sleep quality after applying three conditions: listening to classical music, listening to an audio book and no auditory stimulation. The group that listened to music experienced significantly better sleep quality than the other two groups. In addition, depressive symptoms were reduced. Result.[132]

Tip 2: Wind down. Bring music into your wind-down routine and listen to relaxing music during the hour before bedtime. Try to be present and free of other distractions when listening. Really focus on the sound and be present. Take note of how your sleep changes over a few days. I would recommend Ludovico Einaudi for this, but choose whatever you like. Got a big presentation or meeting coming up? Music has been shown to lessen the psychobiological (mind and body) impact of the stressful event. This study measured the stress response and recovery times (of the autonomic nervous system) after applying a stressor under three conditions: listening to music, listening to the sound of rippling water and no auditory stimulation. The group that listened to music bounced back more quickly than the other groups. So put on some music and smash that presentation. Sure, you'll still be nervous, but you'll thank yourself later.[133]

Tip 3: Showtime. Next time you're faced with a stressful event, such as a presentation or big meeting, listen to some relaxing music for 10 or 20 minutes beforehand. Many of us listen to music that reflects our mood, which is often dictated by our environment, I listen to rap/metal/house in the gym, deep house or classical when relaxing or tropical house in the sun with friends. Music is completely contextual. Rammstein is not a vibe for a family BBQ, but works perfectly before doing a heavy deadlift set. It is often totally dependent on the situation or environment, but music is always available as a tool to boost our mood whenever we need it. Studies have demonstrated that music is actually an effective treatment for depression, anxiety and other neurological disorders.[134] Given that music has the ability to give us a lift during our most difficult times, it can also transport us to different and happier places whenever we need it. If you're having a dull and boring day in the office, then put on 'Sandstorm' by Darude and try not to tap your foot and nod your head. We have this in the locker any time we need it. Just don't forget to plug your headphones in first. I seem to do this with a fair amount of regularity, to everyone's enjoyment – last time I was listening to 'More Than a Woman' by the Bee Gees, too. Cool.

Tip 4: The wellbeing playlist. Build your own wellbeing playlist(s), adding tracks that are helpful to listen to in different moods. It might help to split them out and save the painful surprise of moving from Kygo to System of a Down. When you feel that you might need a mood boost or a calming moment, dip into the playlist and select a song that feels right for the moment. When a friend is struggling with their mental health, it can often be difficult to know what to do to support them. Certainly, we should encourage them to seek professional and clinical help if needed. However, sometimes, sharing a song suggestion can be a way of connecting and letting them know that you are thinking of them when they are low. Plus, as we know, music can alleviate some of the symptoms of depression.

Tip 5: Sharing is caring. Chat to your friend(s) about music when they are in good form. Understand what they are into, because not everyone listens to what you listen to, even if you do have the greatest music taste in the world. If and when they are low, share a song or album you think that they might enjoy listening to. If you want extra brownie points, book tickets to a concert for you to both attend if funds allow. This will give you both something to look forward to. 'Yes, I will go and see Rufus du Sol with you.' Until I spoke to Rob, I literally had no idea that music was quite so powerful. And then he dropped one more knowledge bomb on me. Music can also improve both processing speed and memory, which is why many of us listen to music when we are performing a cognitive task. Studies have identified a number of factors which impact the effectiveness of music in this regard: the listener's enjoyment of the piece of music, the type of music and how musically trained the listener is.[135] Music should not distract the listener from the task, hence less 'musically trained' people would need to select more neutral music. It has to be lyric-less for me, otherwise I start singing and that's not good for my focus, or anyone sitting near me in the office. I can't sit down and concentrate for sustained periods of time without music; it seems to just help my brain feel more relaxed. However, it's always helpful to have the studies to back it up, rather than just the opinion of this bald author, especially when I'm trying to convince you. It wasn't until this year that I was diagnosed with ADHD and received a late diagnosis for dyslexia and dyspraxia in my mid-20s. I feel more creative when I have some music on the go. This whole book has been written while listening to music.

Tip 6: Music flow. Next time you are faced with a cognitive task, try listening to a piece of classical music (or instrumental house – I switch between the two) that you enjoy but doesn't distract you, and enjoy that flow.

Tip 7: Headphones. Lastly, when you are going to do some exercise, don't forget your headphones. Music increases our step and pedal cadence when running and cycling and I am almost certain that it adds a few kilos to your squat, although I have no studies to validate this claim, other than my own, anecdotal, experience.

Many of us are already using music partly to help manage our wellbeing, even if we are not realizing it. However, we can amplify and turn up the benefits a little if we use music more intentionally. Make the playlist, grab your headphones and plug in.

Music is a gift. It feeds the soul. Go forth and feed yours.

Some song recommendations:

Big Love (the Dronez Dub) – Peter Heller
I Wanna Dance With Somebody – Whitney Houston
Ain't Nobody – Chaka Khan
Innerbloom – Rufus du Sol
Lay All Your Love On Me – Abba
L'amour Toujours - Gigi D'Agostino

Movie soundtrack recommendations:

Interstellar – Hans Zimmer
The Last Samurai – Hans Zimmer
Last of the Mohicans – Randy Edelman and Trevor Jones
Pulp Fiction: Music from the Motion Picture Soundtrack

So, my friend, thank you for staying with me for this long; you have nearly made it to the end. I hope you've picked up a thing or two along the way – I certainly have by writing it.

Over the years, what has become clearer and clearer to me is that what works for one person does not work for another and that every single person's needs are different and change over time. You change as you age, your circumstances shift, your tastes mature (supposedly) and subsequently your wellbeing will fluctuate, as will your non-negotiables – the things you need to be your best self.

This is challenging enough for neurotypical people and something we will wrestle with for our entire lives. For the neurodiverse amongst us, this is something else entirely and wellbeing is a whole different beast to be tackled. It is believed that up to 15 per cent of the population is neurodiverse. I told you earlier in the book that I have ADHD, dyslexia and dyspraxia. Neurodiversity is much more common than you would think; according to ADHD Aware, in the UK:

- 8% of people are thought to have ADHD.

- 10% of people are thought to have dyslexia.

- 8% of people are thought to have dyspraxia.

- 6% of people are thought to have dyscalculia.

- 1% of people are thought to have an autistic spectrum condition.

- 1% of people are thought to have Tourette's syndrome.[136]

So I thought to myself, 'this has to be a chapter' and I couldn't think of anyone better than my friend Jess Gosling to chat with about this subject. By day, Jess is a civil servant within the UK Civil Service and by night she is pursuing her PhD in international affairs and is a fully qualified yoga teacher. She has built her career around interdisciplinary thinking, working abroad for over seven years, and with a deep passion for championing belonging and wellbeing in the workplace.

Jess has been recognized globally by being named one of the UK's 'Most Influential Women in Tech' for three years, from 2020 to 2022. In 2022, she was named one of the 'Top 50 Influential Neurodivergent Women' and is simply a wonderful human. Jess has ADHD, autism, OCD, dyslexia, depression and chronic anxiety.

Ryan: Welcome, Jess! Thank you for joining me today to discuss the intersection of neurodiversity and wellbeing. I'm super excited to hear your insights and experiences on this important topic given that I am neurodiverse myself and am on my own personal learning journey. Let's get into it. Prioritizing wellbeing in the modern digital world is increasingly challenging for everyone, but for neurodiverse individuals, it can be even more complex. How do you navigate the pressure to constantly be available in a digital world?

Jess: We should all seek to prioritize our wellbeing; however, doing this in practice can be another thing entirely. In a world where we work more digitally than ever, we can always feel pressure to be 'turned on' and constantly available. This, in and of itself, is a massive barrier to a healthy balance between life and work. If you add neurodiversity, the picture gets even more complicated. Prioritizing your wellbeing (and being neurodiverse) can feel quite alien. It can feel like you can't put yourself first, as everyone else's needs are more important. It can feel selfish to set your own needs first. The reality is that self-care is not selfish. For us to be our best selves, we need to ensure our needs are met, including making time to relax whilst recovering our energy levels.

Ryan: You mentioned that individuals who are neurodiverse may experience feelings of guilt when it comes to prioritizing self-care. How have you personally navigated these feelings?

Jess: People who are neurodiverse may experience a variety of emotions when they understand and ultimately make self-care necessary. Firstly, some people can feel incredible guilt for putting themselves (and equally their needs) over others (so imagine, why are my emotions/feelings more valid?). Secondly, individuals can experience intense feelings of not being deserving enough or 'good enough' to warrant self-care (so imagine, why do I deserve to have self-care?). Thirdly, some people can also struggle with feeling rejected or like an 'outsider', especially in such a productive, driven society (so imagine, what is wrong with me, why do I need to recharge?). These three things are not on the final list, but they are all things I have seen. They are three things I actively struggle with every day. Every single day. I say this as someone balancing a full-time job, a PhD and other fun stuff (like being a yoga teacher, volunteering, etc.). I focus on finding ways to be productive, but not at the expense of my wellbeing. My focus has long been on creating and maintaining a healthy balance between everything work related and a life outside of that.

Here are Jess's and my favourite insights/tips for prioritizing wellbeing as people who are neurodiverse:

Tip 1: Get realistic about your outputs (and do not feel guilty). Every day will be different in terms of energy level, what you can deliver and how you might feel. Productivity should not be at the expense of wellbeing. There is not a sliding scale between productivity and wellbeing – it's not one or the other!

Jess: It can be challenging to feel like you can be productive if you are deflated, paranoid, anxious or have negative mental space. Therefore, it is vital to get realistic about what outputs you can deliver and not feel guilty about it.

Tip 2: Get strategic with your breaks. Take mental breaks during the day, whatever that may look like. Every day is different and we can't always manage all external pressures. However, we can make decisions to prioritize our wellbeing during the day. Mental breaks can mean taking a moment to get some fresh air, speaking to someone close to you on the phone or even popping outside to your nearest cafe to get a coffee. This will help in navigating daily mental fatigue and can help you stay focused.

Tip 3: Take control of your environment. In our busy lives, those who are sensitive to external stimuli can often become overwhelmed by certain situations, locations or environments. They can often feel overwhelmed by sensory things, like bright lights or the vibe in a place. At the same time, they face several challenges regarding how they work and study, having specific preferences. As such, it is crucial to control the environment where possible to mitigate any potentially disturbing/negative stimuli.

Jess: Regarding applicability, I seek to find adjustments as far as possible to ensure I get the support I need. I prefer going somewhere active, like a coffee shop with the energy and vibes and all of that stuff, so tapping into what you know works for you is an excellent practice to get into.

Tip 4: Connect with others (and talk about your feelings). Making time for connections and speaking to others is vital in prioritizing your wellbeing. Life can often feel lonely and we can run the risk of not talking to anyone all day or even for days at a time (if you are remotely working). For those who are neurodiverse, this isolation can be felt even harder. Proactively speaking to those you have an active connection with will enable you to centre yourself. Engaging with family, friends or others you are close to about how you feel can relieve sensations of seclusion.

Tip 5: Be mindful of energy levels. During the day, check in with yourself, especially concerning your energy levels. Being mindful of how much energy you have, depending on what activities or things you must do is quite powerful. For example, Jess and I get energy from seeing/engaging people in group work. However, we both find organizational/admin work incredibly draining. Asking yourself how you feel throughout the day will allow you to reflect on what is working and not working and reallocate tasks, if needed, to another time.

Tip 6: Prioritize sleep and food. Make sure you are sleeping right. Jess has had insomnia since her teenage years, and she still struggles with it. Her sleep is very much dependent on her mood, the weather and many different factors. She ensures that she eats regularly to regulate her mood. Being autistic, she needs sensory support and even if she is not eating, she finds having something to chew comforting.

Tip 7: Seek to be active. There is something about walking that just makes your brain work. Try your best to be active in some way, shape or form daily and change the scenery for at least half an hour per day. Jess does what she feels like on the day and doesn't force it. This positively affects her mood levels and overall positive feelings. She prefers to be active first thing in the morning, even if it's just walking outside around the block. I am very much the same, although I have to walk at lunch and then again when the day is finished. I think I was a greyhound in another life

I really enjoyed chatting with Jess about this and even if you are neurotypical, there is something in here for everyone. I am writing this while in a cafe with some music on; I love the hustle and bustle and it helps me to engage my creative brain. I've written 99.9 per cent of this book in cafes and pubs.

Remember, we all exist on a huge multicoloured spectrum, which makes us all uniquely wonderful and what works for one does not work for another – life would be boring if that were not the case.

CONCLUSION

Here we are, we are at the end of our 52-week journey through the world of wellbeing. Well done for getting this far, I hope you have learned some things along the way.

Here are a few things to remember.

Wellbeing is not something that is to be fixed when broken. There is no app, webinar or training that is coming to save us; rather wellbeing is something we create space for every single day. You are your priority, nothing or no one else. Define your non-negotiables and prioritize them every single day. There is no such thing as work–life balance; it is life, which work is one part of and not the first part. Boundaries first and then balance second.

As we have said time and time again, wellbeing is no small thing, but made up of small things and big doors swing on little hinges. It is the little things that add up to make a huge difference – think of Monsieur Bauby and his 200,000 blinks. If you were to even put 1 per cent of the tips of this book into practice – 2.27 of them – I promise that you will see a huge difference in the not-so-distant future.

It is important not to chastise yourself too much if you falter and fall on your wellbeing journey, because I promise you, you will – it's just a matter of when. This is a lifelong pursuit, not something that is ever achieved. Some weeks you will feel like you have mastered the art of wellbeing, while others might feel like you are walking with cement boots on. But armed with the knowledge, tips and tricks gained from this guide, you have the power to navigate those challenges with a smile. Get back on the horse tomorrow and start again – fresh start. Remember, no one is looking at what you are doing anyway, they are too worried about themselves – as you are, you narcissist, you.

You're not as weird or terrible as you think you are. Everyone is making it up as they go along; some are just better at hiding it. If you want to make a real difference in the world, to smash the stigma that remains around wellbeing (more specifically, mental health) in the workplace and in society, then I suggest that you be honest about how you are feeling, tell people about your struggles, embrace your (so-called) imperfections and wear them proudly. Think about kintsugi and how golden and strong you are now as a result of what you have been through. Helping one person might not change the world, but it may change the world for that one person (the first storytelling is the hardest; it gets easier every single time afterwards). You got this.

That being said, if you have found any of these tips helpful, please pass them on; the more the merrier! This is the key to creating organizations where people can thrive and wellbeing is a priority rather than it being an afterthought; it needs to be a collective effort. It's all well and good if you cut your meetings to finish 5 or 10 minutes early, but if no one else does it and your manager keeps putting 30-minute or one-hour invites in your calendar, then it is a bit pointless really. Share, share, share and make it fun. If it is another onerous initiative, it will go as well as they went. Life and work are very serious, but this doesn't need to be the case. Ask yourself: 'What would Fergus do?'

NOTES

1. Schmich, M (1997) Advice, like youth, probably just wasted on the young, *Chicago Tribune*, 1 June, www.chicagotribune.com/columns/chi-schmich-sunscreen-column-column.html (archived at https://perma.cc/Q3Y4-77TK)

2. Gallup (2023) State of the Global Workplace, www.gallup.com/workplace/349484/state-of-the-global-workplace.aspx (archived at https://perma.cc/7UU7-B7CY)

3. Indeed and Forrester Consulting (2023) The Impact of Workplace Wellbeing and How To Foster It, www.indeed.com/career-advice/career-development/workplace-wellbeing (archived at https://perma.cc/8DYY-ANAQ)

4. Microsoft (2021)The next great disruption is hybrid work – are we ready? www.microsoft.com/en-us/worklab/work-trend-index/hybrid-work (archived at https://perma.cc/Z72X-SBAL)

5. Gallup (2023) Gallup Global Emotions Report, www.gallup.com/analytics/349280/gallup-global-emotions-report.aspx (archived at https://perma.cc/BK8D-5ZRM)

6. Gallup (2023) Gallup Global Emotions Report, www.gallup.com/analytics/349280/gallup-global-emotions-report.aspx (archived at https://perma.cc/BK8D-5ZRM)

7. NHSBSA (2022) Medicines used in mental health – England – quarterly summary statistics April to June 2022, www.nhsbsa.nhs.uk/statistical-collections/medicines-used-mental-health-england/medicines-used-mental-health-england-quarterly-summary-statistics-april-june-2022 (archived at https://perma.cc/2D2J-FTMZ)

8   NHSBSA (2022) Medicines used in mental health – England
    – quarterly summary statistics April to June 2022,
    www.nhsbsa.nhs.uk/statistical-collections/medicines-used-
    mental-health-england/medicines-used-mental-health-england-
    quarterly-summary-statistics-april-june-2022 (archived at
    https://perma.cc/2D2J-FTMZ)

9   NHSBSA (2022) Medicines used in mental health – England
    – quarterly summary statistics April to June 2022, www.
    nhsbsa.nhs.uk/statistical-collections/medicines-used-mental-
    health-england/medicines-used-mental-health-england-
    quarterly-summary-statistics-april-june-2022 (archived at
    https://perma.cc/2D2J-FTMZ)

10 NHSBSA (2022) Medicines used in mental health – England
    – quarterly summary statistics April to June 2022, www.
    nhsbsa.nhs.uk/statistical-collections/medicines-used-mental-
    health-england/medicines-used-mental-health-england-
    quarterly-summary-statistics-april-june-2022 (archived at
    https://perma.cc/2D2J-FTMZ)

11 Office for National Statistics (2023) Measures of national
    well-being dashboard: quality of life in the UK, www.ons.gov.
    uk/peoplepopulationandcommunity/wellbeing/articles/
    measuresofnationalwellbeingdashboardqualityoflifeintheuk/
    2022-08-12 (archived at https://perma.cc/6SMF-N5GM)

12 Kerai, Al (2023) Cell phone usage statistics: mornings are for
    notifications, Reviews.org (archived at https://perma.cc/
    G4VN-WVZK). www.reviews.org/mobile/cell-phone-addiction/
    (archived at https://perma.cc/QB23-M6X3)

13 Office for National Statistics (2023) Measures of national
    well-being dashboard: quality of life in the UK, www.ons.gov.uk/
    peoplepopulationandcommunity/wellbeing/articles/
    measuresofnationalwellbeingdashboardqualityoflifeintheuk/
    2022-08-12 (archived at https://perma.cc/6SMF-N5GM)

14 Ceci, L(2022) Number of apps available in leading app stores
    as of 3rd quarter 2022, Statista, www.statista.com/statistics/

276623/number-of-apps-available-in-leading-app-stores/ (archived at https://perma.cc/7S3G-PKSZ)

[15] Kent, C (2021), Digital health app market booming, finds IQVIA report, Medical Device Network, www.medicaldevice-network.com/news/digital-health-apps/ (archived at https://perma.cc/D5XL-JHXL)

[16] Clear, J (2018) *Atomic Habits*, Avery

[17] Versus Arthritis (2023)The State of Musculoskeletal Health, www.versusarthritis.org/about-arthritis/data-and-statistics/ the-state-of-musculoskeletal-health/ (archived at https://perma.cc/6N5K-QW29)

[18] Hargrave, S (2020) How to take back control of your notifications and get things done, Wired, www.wired.co.uk/ article/control-notifications (archived at https://perma.cc/ UL7P-VRW9)

[19] Asurion (2022) The new normal: phone use is up nearly 4-fold since 2019, according to tech care company Asurion, www.asurion.com/connect/news/tech-usage/ (archived at https://perma.cc/VLQ9-HS4P)

[20] McLaughlin, B, Gotlieb, MR and Mills, DJ (2022) Caught in a dangerous world: problematic news consumption and its relationship to mental and physical ill-being, *Health Communication*, 23 August

[21] Ridley, M (2011) *Rational Optimist: How prosperity evolves*, Fourth Estate, London

[22] Kemp, S (2022) Digital 2022: Time spent using connected tech continues to rise, DataReportal, https://datareportal.com/ reports/digital-2022-time-spent-with-connected-tech (archived at https://perma.cc/QN39-QQDJ)

[23] Flexioffices (2020) Why taking a lunchbreak is good for your health (2020) www.flexioffices.co.uk/blog/why-lunchbreak-is-good-for-your-health%20 (archived at https://perma.cc/ K24X-MRSZ)

[24] Robinson, B (2020), How remote workers can recognize burnout and 6 actions to take, Forbes, www.forbes.com/sites/bryanrobinson/2020/09/06/how-remote-workers-can-recognize-burnout-and-6-actions-to-take/?sh=1528e5294326 (archived at https://perma.cc/4G6X-38ZD)

[25] Aksoy, CG et al (2023) Here's how much commuting time we save when working from home, World Economic Forum, www.weforum.org/agenda/2023/01/commuting-time-save-working-from-home-pandemic/ (archived at https://perma.cc/F5EF-BWZN)

[26] World Health Organization (2022) Musculoskeletal health, www.who.int/news-room/fact-sheets/detail/musculoskeletal-conditions (archived at https://perma.cc/AM5Q-4RFP)

[27] Riggio, RE (2012), There's magic in your smile, *Psychology Today*, www.psychologytoday.com/intl/blog/cutting-edge-leadership/201206/there-s-magic-in-your-smile (archived at https://perma.cc/9L8A-UAQG)

[28] Association for Psychological Science (2012) Grin and bear it! Smiling facilitates stress recovery, www.psychologicalscience.org/news/releases/smiling-facilitates-stress-recovery.html (archived at https://perma.cc/DV3U-952A)

[29] University of Southern California (2015) Thinking vs feeling: the psychology of advertising, https://appliedpsychologydegree.usc.edu/blog/thinking-vs-feeling-the-psychology-of-advertising/ (archived at https://perma.cc/D862-CYGK)

[30] Weissbourd, R, et al (2021) Loneliness in America: How the pandemic has deepened an epidemic of loneliness and what we can do about it, Harvard University, https://mcc.gse.harvard.edu/reports/loneliness-in-america (archived at https://perma.cc/K7BF-ZU9F)

[31] Patel, A and Plowman, S (2022) The increasing importance of a best friend at work, Gallup, www.gallup.com/workplace/397058/increasing-importance-best-friend-work.aspx (archived at https://perma.cc/Z48R-6LJC)

[32] Patel, A and Plowman, S (2022) The increasing importance of a best friend at work, Gallup, www.gallup.com/workplace/397058/increasing-importance-best-friend-work.aspx (archived at https://perma.cc/Z48R-6LJC)

[33] Clear, J (2018) *Atomic Habits*, Avery

[34] Strauss, D (2022), Will anything revive UK productivity? *Financial Times*, www.ft.com/content/8d7ef9b2-24b4-11ea-9a4f-963f0ec7e134 (archived at https://perma.cc/EU4R-UAUK)

[35] Teevan, J, et al (2022), Microsoft New Future of Work Report 2022, Microsoft, www.microsoft.com/en-us/research/uploads/prod/2022/04/Microsoft-New-Future-of-Work-Report-2022.pdf (archived at https://perma.cc/BZT2-BXYQ)

[36] Aksoy, CG et al (2023) Here's how much commuting time we save when working from home, World Economic Forum, www.weforum.org/agenda/2023/01/commuting-time-save-working-from-home-pandemic/ (archived at https://perma.cc/F5EF-BWZN)

[37] Newport, C (2019) *Digital Minimalism*, Portfolio

[38] Diffey, BL (2011) An overview analysis of the time people spend outdoors, *British Journal of Dermatology*, https://pubmed.ncbi.nlm.nih.gov/21128911/ (archived at https://perma.cc/4877-ZPHS)

[39] White, MP et al (2019) Spending at least 120 minutes a week in nature is associated with good health and wellbeing, *Scientific Reports*, **9**, 7730

[40] Turunen, AW et al (2022) Cross-sectional associations of different types of nature exposure with psychotropic, antihypertensive and asthma medication, *Occupational and Environmental Medicine*, **80**, pp 111–18

[41] Lee, MS, Lee, J, Park, BJ and Miyazaki, Y (2015) Interaction with indoor plants may reduce psychological and physiological stress by suppressing autonomic nervous system activity in young adults: a randomized crossover study, Journal of Physiological Anthropology, **34** (1), p 21

42 Pressfield, S (2002) *War of Art: Break through the blocks and win your inner creative battles*, Black Irish, Dublin

43 Pielot, M, Church, K and de Oliveira, R (2014) An in-situ study of mobile phone notifications. In Proceedings of the 16th international conference on human-computer interaction with mobile devices & services (MobileHCI '14), Association for Computing Machinery, New York, NY, USA, pp 233–42

44 Arusion (2022) The new normal: Phone use is up nearly 4-fold since 2019, according to tech care company Asurion (2022), www.asurion.com/connect/news/tech-usage/ (archived at https://perma.cc/VLQ9-HS4P)

45 Stephenson, N (2022) *Why I Am a Bad Correspondent*, www.nealstephenson.com/why-i-am-a-bad-correspondent.html (archived at https://perma.cc/GLX9-RB63)

46 Gilovich, T et al (2000) The spotlight effect in social judgment: an egocentric bias in estimates of the salience of one's own actions and appearance, *Journal of Personality and Social Psychology*, **78** (2) pp 211–22

47 Gilovich, T et al (2002) The spotlight effect revisited: overestimating the manifest variability of our own actions and appearance, *Journal of Experimental Social Psychology*, **38**, pp 93–99

48 Lewsley, J (2022) Tired in winter? Here's the science behind seasonal fatigue, Livescience, www.livescience.com/tired-in-winter-the-science-behind-seasonal-fatigue (archived at https://perma.cc/QPG9-FTRX)

49 Mind (2022) Seasonal affective disorder, www.mind.org.uk/information-support/types-of-mental-health-problems/seasonal-affective-disorder-sad/about-sad/ (archived at https://perma.cc/72HV-RPST)

50 World Happiness Report (2022) World Happiness Report, https://worldhappiness.report/ed/2022/ (archived at https://perma.cc/2HFF-KU78)

51 Wiking, M (2016) *The Little Book of Hygge: The Danish way to live well*, Penguin, London

52 Nelson, D (2022), Hygge: The Danish secret to happiness, Redefiners, www.redefinerswl.org/post/hygge-the-danish-secret-to-happiness (archived at https://perma.cc/5445-LV6J)

53 Fang, R (2020) *An Ecological Approach to Obesity and Eating Disorders*, Clemson University, Clemson

54 Nicholls, K (2022) Key statistics about men and mental health, Counselling Directory, www.counselling-directory.org.uk/men-and-mental-health-stats.html (archived at https://perma.cc/HDC9-LVBM)

55 ABS (2022) National Study of Mental Health and Wellbeing, 2020–21, www.abs.gov.au/statistics/health/mental-health/national-study-mental-health-and-wellbeing/2020-21 (archived at https://perma.cc/4UJU-NF9C)

56 National Institute of Mental Health (nd) Agoraphobia, www.nimh.nih.gov/health/statistics/agoraphobia (archived at https://perma.cc/YVQ9-GMTQ)

57 Clear, J (2018) *Atomic Habits: An easy and proven way to build good habits and break bad ones*, Random House Business, London

58 Stulberg, B (2019) Show up. Mood follows action, Medium, https://bstulberg.medium.com/show-up-mood-follows-action-943469d43480 (archived at https://perma.cc/T79U-2YBL)

59 Sagan, C (1977) *The Dragons of Eden*, Random House, New York

60 McGee, B (2010) *The Story of Philosophy*, DK Books, London

61 Burkeman, O (2022), Four Thousand Weeks, Vintage, London

62 Pirsig, R (1991) *Zen and the Art of Motorcycle Maintenance*, Vintage, London

63 Parrish, S (2023), Clear thinking, FS, https://fs.blog/brain-food/april-2-2023/ (archived at https://perma.cc/ZB2F-5LY2)

64 Leahy, R (2005) *The Worry Cure*, Harmony/Rodale, New York

65 Tremblay, M (2021) What many people misunderstand about the stoic dichotomy of control, *Modern Stoiscism*, https://modernstoicism.com/what-many-people-misunderstand-

about-the-stoic-dichotomy-of-control-by-michael-tremblay/
(archived at https://perma.cc/HY4T-X62D)

[66] Schmich, M (1997) Advice, like youth, probably just wasted on
the young, *Chicago Tribune*, 1 June, www.chicagotribune.com/
columns/chi-schmich-sunscreen-column-column.html (archived
at https://perma.cc/Q3Y4-77TK)

[67] Raven, P (2022) How many Britons have made New Year's
resolutions for 2023?, YouGov, 28 December, https://yougov.
co.uk/topics/society/articles-reports/2022/12/28/how-many-
britons-have-made-new-years-resolutions-2 (archived at
https://perma.cc/4VD8-A6ZC)

[68] Microsoft (2022) The rise of the triple peak day,
www.microsoft.com/en-us/worklab/triple-peak-day (archived at
https://perma.cc/9R59-GCCA)

[69] Microsoft (2021) Research proves your brain needs breaks,
www.microsoft.com/en-us/worklab/work-trend-index/brain-
research (archived at https://perma.cc/K6KE-X7YB)

[70] Thompson, D (2022) This is what happens when there are too
many meetings, *The Atlantic*, 4 April, www.theatlantic.com/
newsletters/archive/2022/04/triple-peak-day-work-from-
home/629457/ (archived at https://perma.cc/Y6WT-K8ZV)

[71] Samiri, I and Millard, S (2022) Why is UK productivity low
and how can it improve?, NIESR, 26 September, www.niesr.ac.
uk/blog/why-uk-productivity-low-and-how-can-it-improve
(archived at https://perma.cc/W42K-EZF7)

[72] Global Web Index (2018) Fear of missing out (FOMO) on
social media, www.gwi.com/hubfs/Downloads/Fear-of-Missing-
Out-on-Social-Media-report.pdf (archived at https://perma.cc/
M9JE-HLE5)

[73] Heitmann, B (2018) Your workplace guide to summer vacation,
LinkedIn Official Blog, 11 July, https://blog.linkedin.com/2018/
july/11/your-workplace-guide-to-summer-vacation (archived at
https://perma.cc/NYF6-GY8X)

74 Heitmann, B (2018) Your workplace guide to summer vacation, LinkedIn Official Blog, 11 July, https://blog.linkedin.com/2018/july/11/your-workplace-guide-to-summer-vacation (archived at https://perma.cc/NYF6-GY8X)

75 Harris, M (2017) *Solitude: In pursuit of a singular life in a crowded world*, Random House, New York

76 Petric, D (2022) The introvert-ambivert-extrovert spectrum, *Open Journal of Medical Psychology*, **11**, pp 103–11

77 Parish, S (2022) The art of being alone, FS, https://fs.blog/being-alone/ (archived at https://perma.cc/2G32-GHTH)

78 Clifford, C (2019) Bill Gates took solo 'think weeks' in the woods – why it's a great strategy, CNBC, 28 July, www.cnbc.com/2019/07/26/bill-gates-took-solo-think-weeks-in-a-cabin-in-the-woods.html (archived at https://perma.cc/2D5C-NQ9N)

79 Weiner, J (2013) The importance of scheduling nothing, LinkedIn, 3 April, www.linkedin.com/pulse/20130403215758-22330283-the-importance-of-scheduling-nothing/ (archived at https://perma.cc/K3T6-VFNP)

80 Schmich, M (1997) Advice, like youth, probably just wasted on the young, *Chicago Tribune*, 1 June, www.chicagotribune.com/columns/chi-schmich-sunscreen-column-column.html (archived at https://perma.cc/Q3Y4-77TK)

81 Kaufman, PD (2005) *Poor Charlie's Almanack: The wit and wisdom of Charles T Munger*, Donning Company, Brookfield

82 Sivers, D (2019) How to ask your mentors for help, Derek Sivers, 17 October, https://sive.rs/ment (archived at https://perma.cc/WWS3-CRCW)

83 Ryan, RM et al (2010) Vitalizing effects of being outdoors and in nature, *Journal of Environmental Psychology*, **30** (2)

84 Wild, S (2022) Is cold water therapy good for you?, Bupa, 22 June, www.bupa.co.uk/newsroom/ourviews/cold-water-therapy (archived at https://perma.cc/7GH9-HTHA)

85 Massey, H et al (2020) Mood and well-being of novice open water swimmers and controls during an introductory outdoor

swimming programme: A feasibility study, *Lifestyle Medicine*,
1 (2)

[86] Kopplin, CS and Rosenthal, L (2022) The positive effects of
combined breathing techniques and cold exposure on perceived
stress: a randomised trial, *Current Psychology*

[87] Walker, M (2018) *Why we sleep: the new science of sleep and
dreams*, Penguin, London

[88] Cappuccio, FP, D'Elia, L, Strazzullo, P and Miller, MA (2010)
Sleep duration and all-cause mortality: a systematic review and
meta-analysis of prospective studies, *Sleep*, **33** (5)

[89] Soong, J (2010) The secret (and surprising) power of naps,
WedMD, www.webmd.com/balance/features/the-secret-and-
surprising-power-of-naps (archived at https://perma.cc/4SEF-
AE99)

[90] Frankl, VE (1992) *Man's search for meaning: An introduction
to logotherapy*, Beacon Press, Boston

[91] Steger, M, Kashdan, T and Oishi, S (2008) Being good by doing
good: Daily eudaimonic activity and well-being, *Journal of
Research in Personality*, **42**, pp 22–42

[92] Krockow, EM (2018) How many decisions do we make each
day, *Psychology Today*, 27 September, www.psychologytoday.
com/gb/blog/stretching-theory/201809/how-many-decisions-do-
we-make-each-day (archived at https://perma.cc/82Y8-HH7A)

[93] Kleiner, K (2011) Lunchtime leniency: judges' rulings are
harsher when they are hungrier, *Scientific American*, 1
September, www.scientificamerican.com/article/lunchtime-
leniency/ (archived at https://perma.cc/4N5T-VV4P)

[94] Iyer, GR., Blut, M, Xiao, SH and Grewal, D (2019) Impulse
buying: a meta-analytic review, *Journal of the Academy of
Marketing Science*, **48**, pp 384–404

[95] Dweck, Carol S et al (2013) Beliefs about willpower determine
the impact of glucose on self-control, *PNAS*, **110** (37)

[96] Nosen, E and Woody, SR (2014) Acceptance of cravings:
How smoking cessation experiences affect craving beliefs,
Behaviour Research and Therapy, **59**

97 Eyal, N (2020) Willpower is not a limited resource, *Medium*,
    14 January, https://forge.medium.com/this-is-what-most-
    people-get-wrong-about-willpower-72deab39fa59#
    (archived at https://perma.cc/QMS8-C92U)

98 Stone, L (2012) The connected life: from email apnea to
    conscious computing, *Huffpost*, 7 July, www.huffpost.com/
    entry/email-apnea-screen-apnea_b_1476554?guccounter=1
    (archived at https://perma.cc/882B-6DSZ)

99 Naragon, K (2018) We still love email, but we're spreading the
    love with other channels, Adobe, 21 August, https://business.
    adobe.com/blog/perspectives/love-email-but-spreading-the-
    love-other-channels (archived at https://perma.cc/FTT4-QMZT)

100 Madore, KP and Wagner, AD (2019) Multicosts of
    multitasking, Dana Foundation, 5 April, www.dana.org/article/
    multicosts-of-multitasking/ (archived at https://perma.cc/
    CD3U-U4CQ)

101 Parikh, K (2022) The cost of context switching, *The Transcript*,
    13 July, www.loom.com/blog/cost-of-context-switching
    (archived at https://perma.cc/4KB8-KXAE)

102 Montini, L (2014), The high cost of multitasking, *Inc.*,
    27 June, www.inc.com/laura-montini/infographic/the-high-
    cost-of-multitasking.html (archived at https://perma.cc/8MN5-
    3TP5)

103 Mark, G (2008) The cost of interrupted work: more speed and
    stress, Conference: Proceedings of the 2008 Conference on
    Human Factors in Computing Systems, Florence, Italy

104 Neal, DT, Wood, W and Quinn, JM (2006) Habits – a repeat
    performance, *Current Directions in Psychological Science*,
    15 (4), pp 198–202

105 Duhigg, C (2013) *The Power of Habit*, Penguin, London

106 Hobson, N (2023) People and really successful people. What
    separates the two, *Inc.*, 31 March, www.inc.com/nick-hobson/
    warren-buffett-there-are-successful-people-really-successful-
    people-what-separates-two.html (archived at https://perma.cc/
    S4MB-YTMN)

107 Holiday, R (2023) All success is a lagging indicator, RyanHoliday.net, https://ryanholiday.net/all-success-is-a-lagging-indicator/ (archived at https://perma.cc/J86M-JPZD)

108 Cho, A (2021) 1 in 400 trillion, *Muddyum*, 23 June, https://muddyum.net/1-in-400-trillion-3174b5c67adb (archived at https://perma.cc/F4GA-GAZK)

109 Wiseman, R, (2004) *The Luck Factor*, Arrow, London

110 Kondo, M (2014) *The Life-Changing Magic of Tidying Up*, Ten Speed Press

111 Broadley, J, et al (2023) The Workplace Health Report, Champion Health, https://championhealth.co.uk/insights/guides/workplace-health-report/ (archived at https://perma.cc/M8T2-V3NR)

112 Gielan, M (2015) *Broadcasting Happiness*, BenBella Books, Dallas

113 Lyubomirsky, S (2010) *The How of Happiness*, Piatkus, London

114 Paiella, G (2021) The brain-changing magic of new experiences, *GQ*, 27 May, www.gq.com/story/brain-changing-magic-new-experiences (archived at https://perma.cc/7KPM-3ST9)

115 Schmich, M (1997) Advice, like youth, probably just wasted on the young, *Chicago Tribune*, 1 June, www.chicagotribune.com/columns/chi-schmich-sunscreen-column-column.html (archived at https://perma.cc/Q3Y4-77TK)

116 Lee, A (2020) Why you really shouldn't be eating lunch at your desk, *WIRED*, 10 January, www.wired.co.uk/article/eating-lunch-at-your-desk-health (archived at https://perma.cc/5WMR-6LNC)

117 Tulshyan, R (2021) Take your lunch break! *Harvard Business Review*, 21 January, https://hbr.org/2021/01/take-your-lunch-break# (archived at https://perma.cc/RD94-S8UF)

118 Workthere (2018) The average UK lunch hour is just 34 minutes – how can the office change this? 6 September, www.workthere.com/en-gb/news-guides/news/the-average-uk-

lunch-hour-press-release/ (archived at https://perma.cc/
F2M9-VTAT)

[119] Rao, S (2016) The 9 environments that make up your life,
Medium, https://medium.com/the-mission/the-9-environments-
that-make-up-your-life-357d23f4a8af (archived at
https://perma.cc/FYJ3-CUQ8)

[120] Wen, T (2018) What workers around the world do for lunch,
Worklife, www.bbc.com/worklife/article/20180110-what-
workers-around-the-world-do-for-lunch (archived at
https://perma.cc/B5UU-REYA)

[121] Minett, C (2023) The British 'tea and biscuit break' is slowly
becoming a thing of the past, 3AddedMinutes, 12 April,
www.3addedminutes.com/read-this/the-british-tea-and-biscuit-
break-is-slowly-becoming-a-thing-of-the-past-4101685
(archived at https://perma.cc/T5Z4-98L5)

[122] Deloitte (2023) 2023 Gen Z and Millennial Survey,
www.deloitte.com/global/en/issues/work/content/
genzmillennialsurvey.html (archived at https://perma.cc/
9HML-7FGE)

[123] Fleming, W (2023) Estimating effects of individual-level
workplace mental wellbeing interventions: cross-sectional
evidence from the UK, Wellbeing Research Centre

[124] Lewis, L (2021) Workplace wellbeing insights from the 2021
world happiness report, Indeed, 20 March, www.indeed.com/
lead/workplace-well-being-study-insights (archived at
https://perma.cc/UN8F-Z25N)

[125] Popper, KR (1963) *Conjectures and Refutations*, Routledge,
London

[126] Oberman, HA (1969) Early history of blood substitutes:
transfusion of milk, *Transfusion*, 9, pp 74–77

[127] Broadley, J et al (2023) The Workplace Health Report,
Champion Health, https://championhealth.co.uk/insights/
guides/workplace-health-report/ (archived at https://perma.cc/
M8T2-V3NR)

[128] Money & Pensions Service (2021) 24 million UK adults don't feel confident managing their money. Talk Money Week is here to help, www.maps.org.uk/2021/11/10/24-million-uk-adults-dont-feel-confident-managing-their-money-talk-money-week-is-here-to-help/ (archived at https://perma.cc/U8C9-DGQC)

[129] O'Brien, L (2023) UK savings statistics 2023, Money.co.uk, www.money.co.uk/savings-accounts/savings-statistics (archived at https://perma.cc/G9Z2-H2YW)

[130] Nielsen (2015) Everyone listens to music, but how we listen is changing, www.nielsen.com/insights/2015/everyone-listens-to-music-but-how-we-listen-is-changing/ (archived at https://perma.cc/D9PD-E44L)

[131] Onieva-Zafra, MD et al (2013) Effect of music as nursing intervention for people diagnosed with fibromyalgia, *Pain Management Nursing*, **14** (2) 2013

[132] Harmat, L, Takács, J and Bódizs, R (2008) Music improves sleep quality in students. *Journal of Advanced Nursing*, **62** (3) pp 327–35

[133] Thoma, MV, La Marca, R, Brönnimann, R, Finkel, L, Ehlert, U and Nater, UM (2013) The effect of music on the human stress response, *PLoS One*

[134] Raglio, A, Attardo, L, Gontero, G, Rollino, S, Groppo, E and Granieri E (2015) Effects of music and music therapy on mood in neurological patients, *World Journal of Psychiatry*, **5** (1), pp 68–78

[135] Gold, BP et al (2013) Pleasurable music affects reinforcement learning according to the listener, *Frontiers in Psychology*, **4**

[136] ADHD Aware (nd) Neurodevelopmental conditions, https://adhdaware.org.uk/what-is-adhd/neurodiversity-and-other-conditions/ (archived at https://perma.cc/44KQ-KJLY)

Looking for another book?

Explore our award-winning books from global business experts in Skills and Careers

Scan the code to browse

www.koganpage.com/sce

Printed in the USA
CPSIA information can be obtained
at www.ICGtesting.com
JSHW072125020224
56568JS00009B/159